The Photographed Cat

1

Previous Pages:
Ylla
1950's

Above:
Thomas Eakins
Amelia Van Buren and Cat
Undated

THE PHOTOGRAPHED CAT

Edited by Jean-Claude Suarès

Text by Chris Casson Madden

With photographs by:

Barbara Alper
Jim Bengston
John Bryson
Henri Cartier-Bresson
Ed Centner
Susan Chang
Jere Cockrell
William Coupon
Bruce Davidson
Thomas Eakins
Elliott Erwitt
Carl Fisher
Leonard Freed
Harry Frees
Jill Freedman
Terry Gruber
Philippe Halsman
Bill Hayward
Liza Himmel
Armen Kachaturian
Peter B. Kaplan
André Kertesz
Matthew Klein
Jill Krementz
Brian Lav
Anthony Loew
Diane Marino
Antonio Mendoza
Duane Michals
Barbara Morgan
Roy Morsch
Eadweard Muybridge
Eleni Milonas
Arnold Newman
Susan Opton
Ruth Orkin
Jean C. Pigozzi
Guy Le Querrec
Priscilla Ratazzi
Lawrence Robins
Jean-Regis Roustan
Eva Rudling
Philippe Salaün
David Seymour
Jane Shreibman
Rick Smolan
Frank Spinelli
Edward Steichen
Harvey Stein
George Tice
Arthur Tress
Carol Weinberg
Harry Warnecke
Dan Wynn
Ylla
and many more.

Doubleday & Co., Inc.
Garden City, New York

Design: J.C. Suarès and Robert Best
Cover: Photograph by Peter B. Kaplan
Production: Nancy Gordon and Robert Best
Research and Permissions: Deborah Augenblick.

ISBN: 0- 385- 17081-5
Library of Congress Catalog Card Number 80-665

Printed in the United States of America
First Edition
Additional copyright information appears on page 126. Any rights information found erroneous or missing will be corrected in future editions.

To Nina Suarès and Kevin Madden in appreciation of their patience and support.

Special thanks to John Cavanaugh (Magnum Photos), Susan Harder, Maria Morris (MOMA) and Rosemary Rinaldi.

Also edited by J.C. Suarès:
The Illustrated Cat (with Seymour Chwast)
The Literary Cat (with Seymour Chwast)
The Literary Dog (with William Maloney)
The Illustrated Horse (with Chuck Stephen)
Flight (with David Owen)
Rocketship (with Robert Malone)
Alien Creatures (with Richard Siegel)
Fantastic Planets (with Richard Siegel)
Art of the Times
Watergate Without Words

Other books written by Chris Casson Madden:
The Summer House Cookbook
The Compleat Lemon

The Photographed Cat

Introduction

ats have nine lives.

The average photographer has a studio, several cameras, a darkroom, an assistant, an answering machine...and a cat. This book is about the friendship between photographers and cats.

The cat made his appearance in art long before the invention of the camera. He was sculpted by the Egyptians thirty centuries ago, and painted for the past thousand years, in Europe as well as in Japan. J.B. Greuze painted cats during the

Harry Whittier Frees
1920's
These animal postcards were collected by hundreds of enthusiastic postcard buffs. They were also found on calendars and children's books. Frees always attributed his results to his kind and patient handling of the animals. When not using his two cats, Rags and Fluff, he borrowed animals from the neighboring farms of Oaks, Pennsylvania.

eighteenth century, Francisco Goya included cats in early nineteenth century etchings, and Pablo Picasso did an etching of a cat in 1942.

By the time the camera was invented, the cat had already (a) found himself in the language of art and (b) become a fixture in the artist's studio. It was only a matter of time before he would stroll in front of the lens.

Early photographers were quick to recognize the photographic possibilities of the cat. As collectors of vintage prints and old postcards will attest the earliest subjects included children, cats, dogs, children with cats, children with dogs, and dogs with cats.

Nearly half a century ago Harry Whittier Frees turned out hundreds of cat postcards for the Rotograph Company. His images depicting kittens in every kind of bizarre situation and in strange hand-made costumes could fill a thirty-volume anthology of kitsch, but neverthless they are sought after like never before by nostalgia buffs.

Serious photographers too,

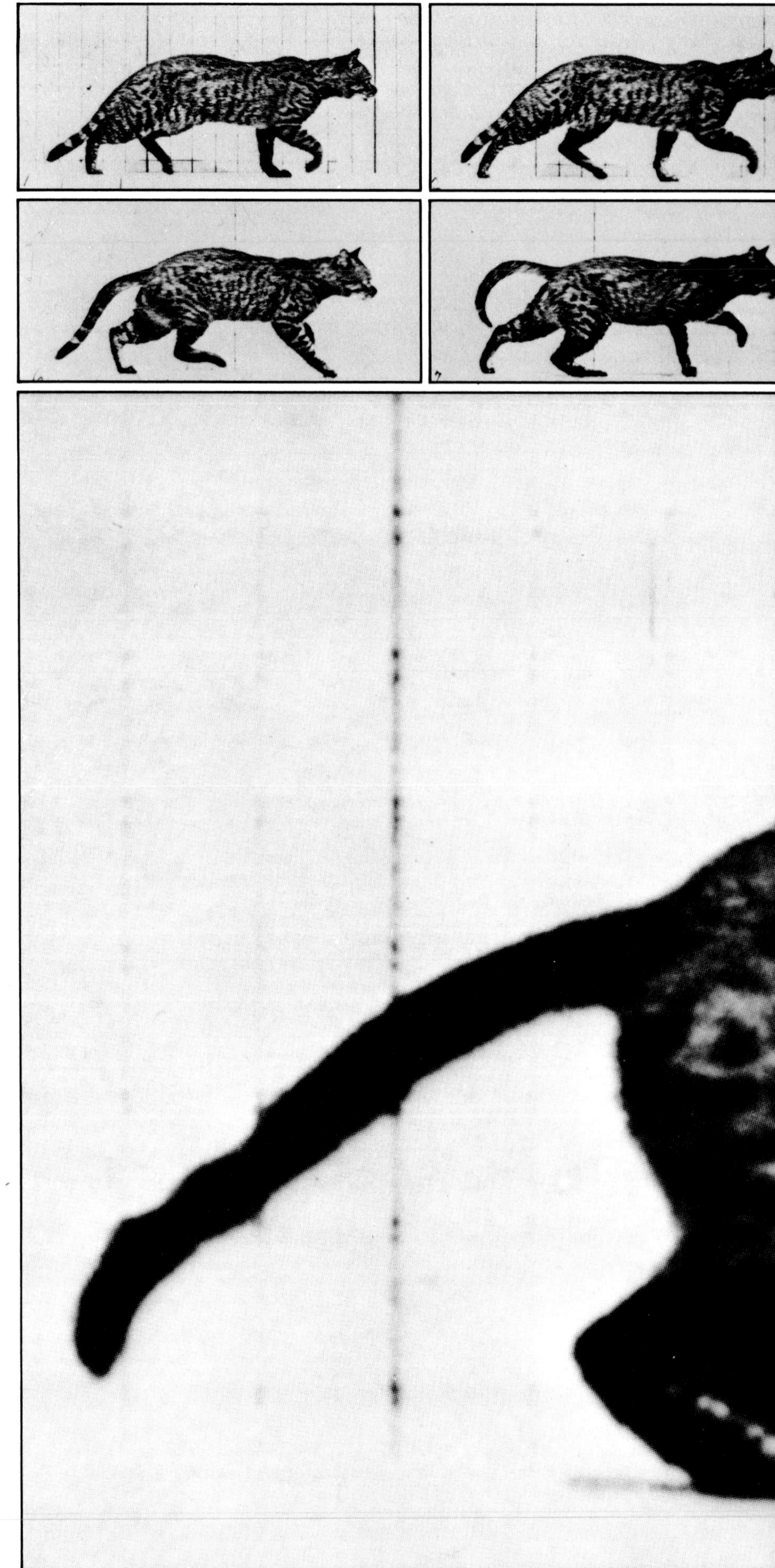

Eadweard Muybridge
Animal Locomotion 717, The Cat
1884
Eadweard Muybridge's classic achievement—developing the moving picture—began in 1882 when he was asked to settle a $25 wager between two millionaires who were arguing about whether a trotting horse could have all four feet off the ground at one time.
Muybridge set up a bank of sequentially triggered cameras, and discovered a new technique for capturing movement in humans and animals.
Inspired by his results, he continued to experiment. And his series of photographs of motion have never since been excelled.

Introduction

like Edward Steichen and Thomas Eakins, visualized the cat as a fitting subject and paid tribute to it. It is hard to say which is the earliest great photograph of a cat, but if we start with the 1880's there is no question that Eadweard Muybridge's classic studies of the movements of cats are the best known. Muybridge studied the movements of people and of dozens of animals and birds as well as cats, his is still the most authoritative work on the subject. Little has been learned about the movement of cats, in the past hundred years, that Muybridge did not discover.

Muybridge built some elaborate sets at the University of Pennsylvania where he conducted his experiments. To show the movement of a cat running, for example, he used as many as a dozen synchronized cameras. The results were published in 1887 under the title *Animal Locomotion.*

Neither the painter nor the sculptor can record the movement of the cat as well as the camera does. Certainly the two examples of cats being

Ylla
Tossed Kittens
1950's

tossed up in the air could not have been accomplished any other way. Ylla and Barbara Morgan, two great women photographers working several years apart, could not resist the temptation to record the cat in mid-air.

Besides recording the beauty of the cat, the camera has also never lost an opportunity to record cats in the news. And because the cat is an inveterate scene-stealer, he never fails to create news in the presence of a camera. Everyday thousands upon thousands of wire service photographs, from just about everywhere in the world, find their way to the desks of newspaper editors. These photos show all types of cats, from the homeliest stray in the back alleys of Rome to the most pampered Angora living high above Park Avenue, stealing some scene or another.

The files of the Associated Press and United Press International are full of examples of cats creating news. At last count they ran two-to-one against pictures of children, five-to-one against pictures of dogs, and

Barbara Morgan
Tossed Cats
1942

ten-to-one against pictures of horses, pigeons and seals. Cats manage to get stuck on top of poles, be rescued from fires, carry kittens across busy thoroughfares—and to be the fattest, or the rarest, or the most expensive in the world.

Today the commercial influence of the cat is all-pervasive. We find cats prominently featured on Christmas cards, calendars, stamps, cigarette packages, and on and on.

Cats have also found their way into advertisements for everything from jewelry to mattresses. They appear there as symbols of independence and mystery. They very seldom appear alongside women, however, because most of the time they are there *instead* of women.

Just as there are high-fashion female models there are highly trained cat models. Some can bring their trainers over $200 per day. Just like great women models they appear on time, they know how to look good, they keep to themselves during breaks, and they never bother to look at the polaroid test-prints

Associated Press
1973
Looking like a "cat on a hot tin roof," this lucky feline suffered only minor injuries in a Seattle rooftop fire. Local firemen rescued her and administered oxygen.

Jill Freedman
Greenwich Village
1972
"This was the picture that got me interested in shooting firemen. Three years later I shot my book, *Firehouse*. He had just saved the cat from a fire that was going on down my block. It was about four or five in the morning, and I had just gotten a flash. It was one of my first flash pictures."

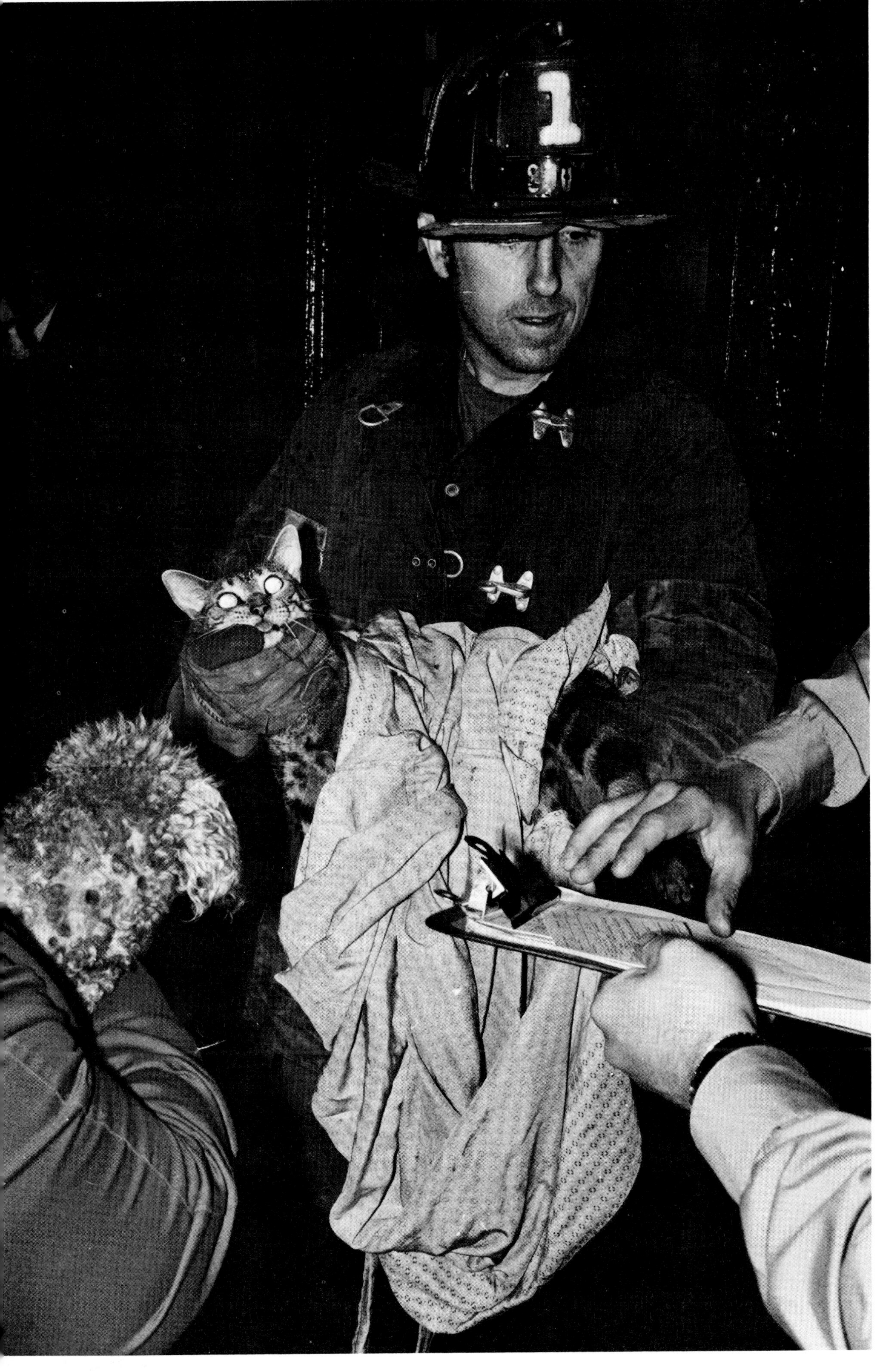
1

Harry Warnecke
New York
1925
This scene actually took place on a warm summer afternoon in 1925. But by the time Harry Warnecke, photographer for the *New York News*, reached Center Street, the mother cat had already carried her kittens across the street and home. Undaunted, Harry set up the shot again and persuaded the policeman to hold up the honking motorists while he handed the cats to a man on one side of the street and the owner called them from the opposite side. It didn't quite work the first time due to some understandable confusion on the part of the mother cat, but, after one more try, Harry had his picture.

The Bettmann Archive
1920's

United Press International
1962

United Press International
1959

Whether laughing, dancing or singing, felines in photographs from stock wire services have always had great appeal for both newspaper editors and readers.

that litter the floor of the studio. They let the account executives, the stylists and the photographers worry, knowing all along that they can look great when they want to.

Once in a while a scruffy nonprofessional makes it to a magazine cover or an advertisement. But you always hear the same reasons for its success—it's either "this cat was always a ham," or "all cats are hams."

The tremendous growth of the cat food industry, and the advertising that promotes it, has given us a whole new breed of superstar cat. Morris the *9-Lives* cat, and probably the most famous of the celebrity cats, made his debut in 1969 and remained active until recently, when his nine lives were suddenly over. (Morris was actually discovered living in one of the "death row" cages at the Humane Society in Hinsdale, Illinois.) His successor has been selected and is carrying the proud mantle with dignity and, of course, the appropriate finickiness.

Cats have also had their fair share of time on the silver

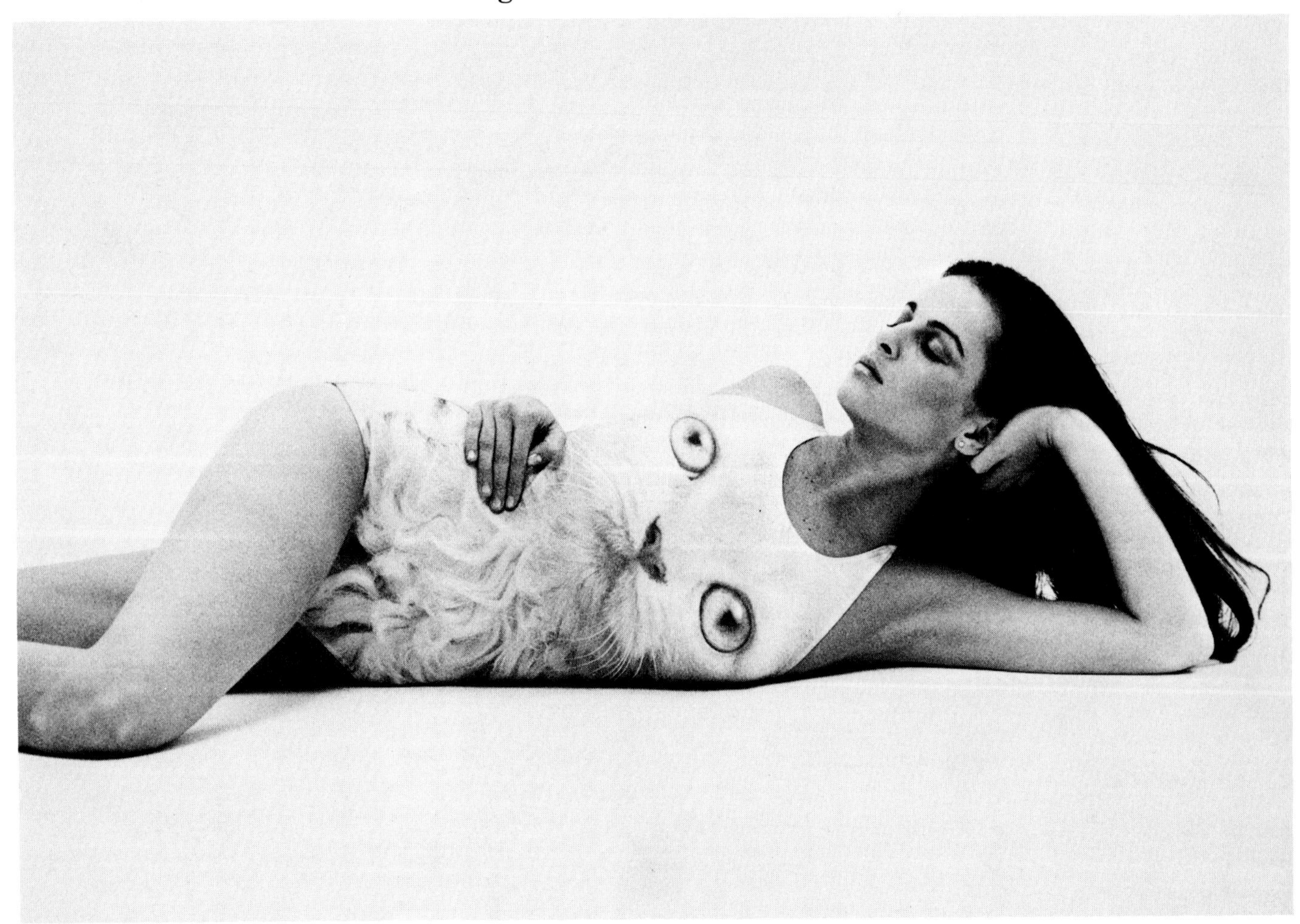

Priscilla Ratazzi
New York
1979
"I took this picture of Sonia Paula Machado, a Brazilian socialite, and showed it to *Interview Magazine* because they're always interested in pretty girls who have names. I found the suit at Fiorucci's."

screen. Many movie directors agree that strays and foundlings very often make the best animal actors. Probably the most famous cat, prior to Morris, was Orangey who could easily have been a stand-in for Morris, their physical similarity being that close.

Orangey, or Rhubarb, as he came to be known to almost everyone, played alongside some big stars in his day. He stole scenes from Ray Milland in *Rhubarb*, from Jackie Gleason in *Gigot*, and from Audrey Hepburn in *Breakfast at Tiffany's*, to mention only a few.

If the celebrity cat has been immortalized in movies and on television, the anonymous cat has been celebrated through the brilliance of some of the world's greatest photographers. Henri Cartier-Bresson's *Shop Window* (pages 40-41) captures the essence of the street cat, while André Kertesz's cat and dog in a butcher shop dramatizes the random poignancy that often exists between cats and other strangers (page 92).

Dan Wynn shot his own kitten, Licorice (pages 84-85),

Roy Morsch
New York
1978
"Cats are creatures that are never the same twice. They have so many moods, so many looks, and so many feelings, and it all comes across on film. This photograph came about by accident. We were cooking a turkey and decided we might as well make a picture of it.... My cat, Broadway, was showing an inordinate amount of interest in the turkey, and so I thought, 'Wow, that's the shot.'"

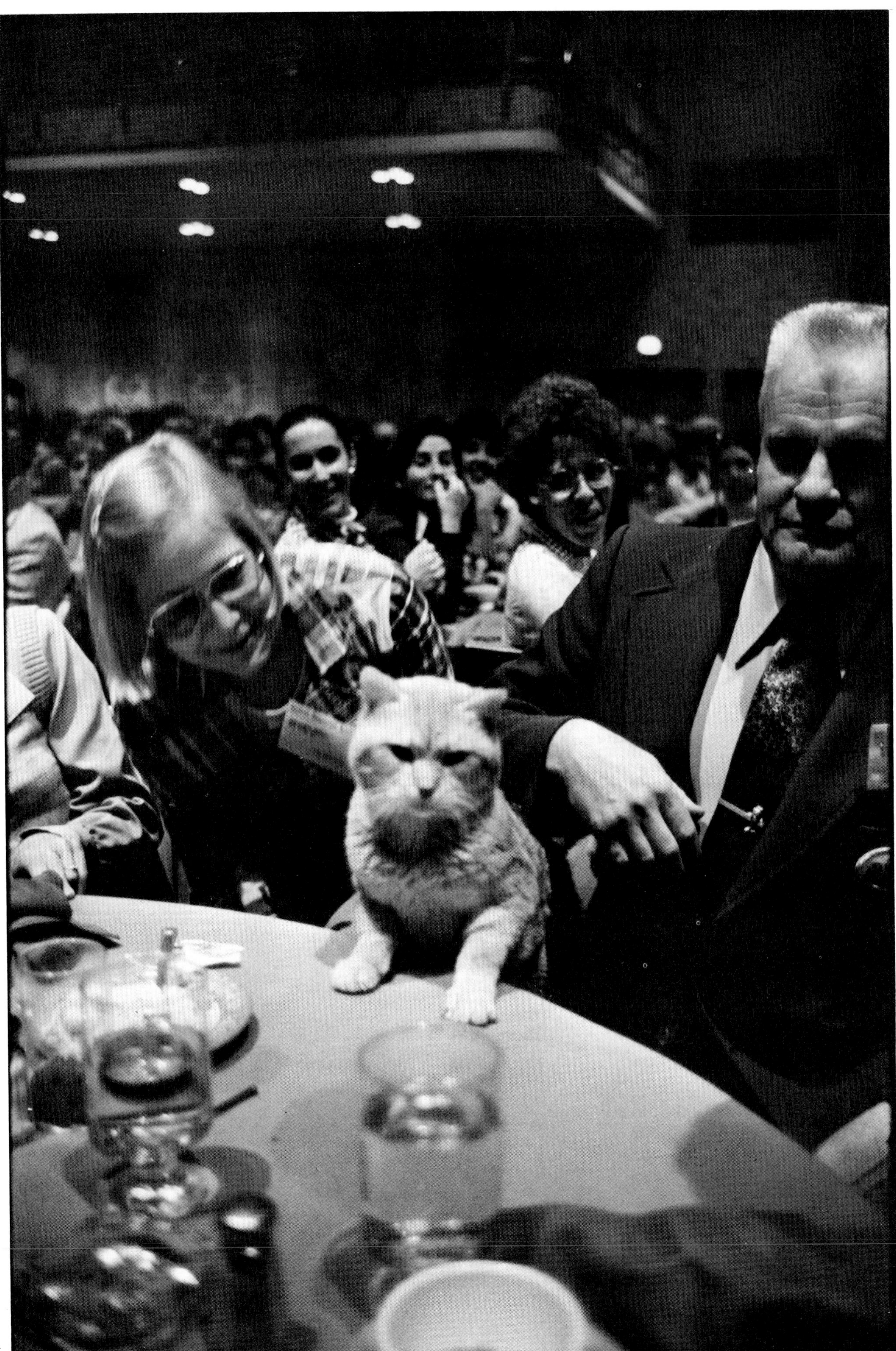

when he surprised her with his camera in his apartment. Jill Freedman, in the course of exploring the streets of New York City while doing a book on firemen, succeeded in capturing the city cat in her photograph (page 31).

The cats of the famous, by their constant proximity to their masters and mistresses, have achieved a stature of their own simply by having been there when the shutter was squeezed. And, from the photographer's point of view, their presence lends an air of humanity to those celebrated subjects.

But whether they're world-renown photographers or wire service neophytes, they all agree on one tenet—you cannot always get a cat to do what you want it to do.

Almost every photographer we spoke to agreed that even under optimum conditions you can't predict the outcome. As one photographer remarked, "Cats are independent. They don't pay attention to you, and they have a mind of their own. They're interested in you for a few seconds, and then they tune

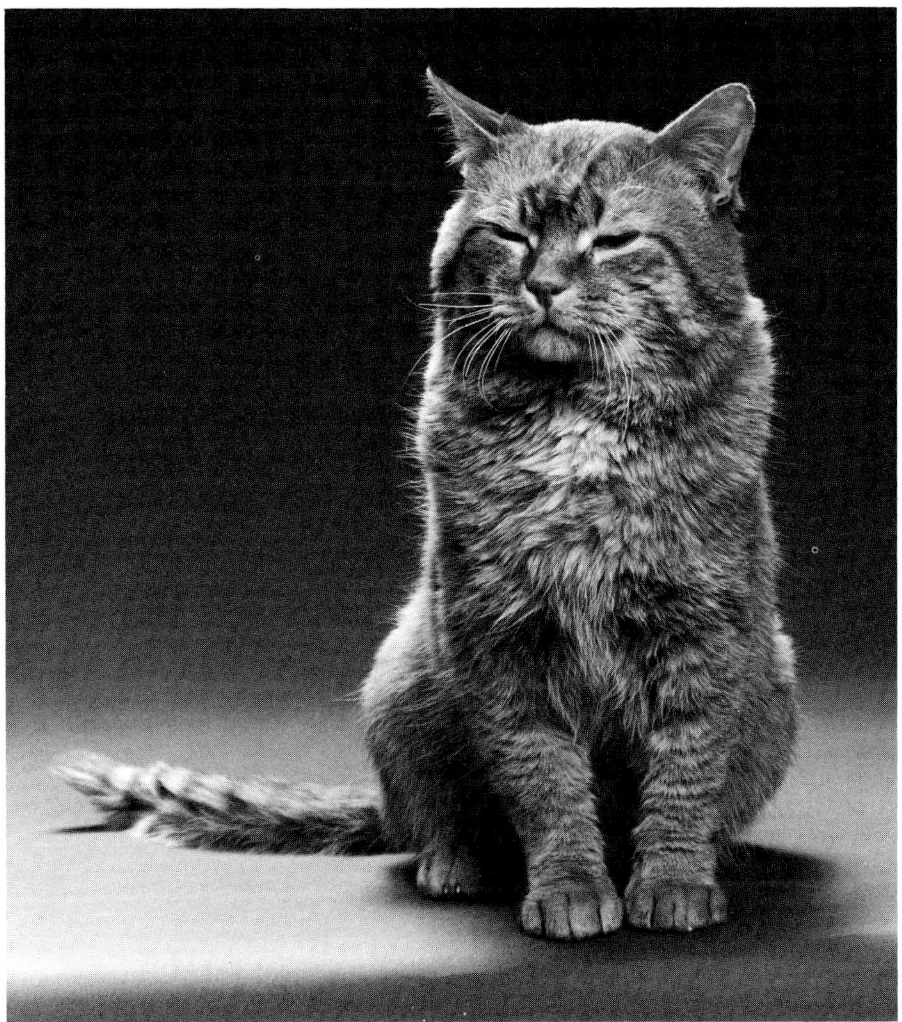

Jill Krementz
Morris
Washington D.C.
1974
Morris the Cat—culinary expert and television star—dining at the American Booksellers Convention.

The new Morris
Designated to carry on the legend and legacy of the original Morris, at left. He beat nearly a hundred other cats to the title, and to a lucrative television contract.

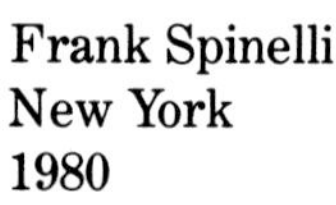

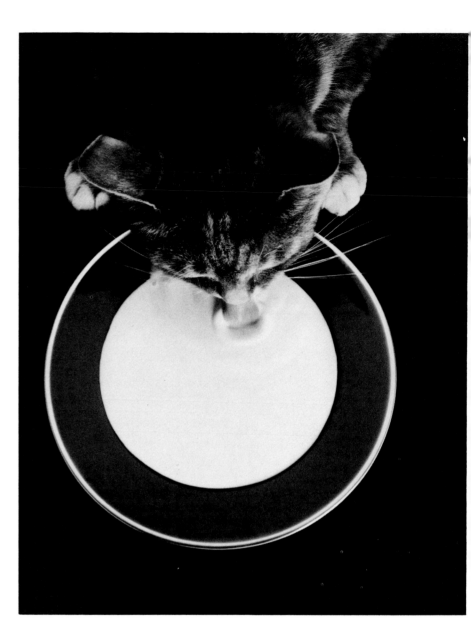

Frank Spinelli
New York
1980
"I wanted to add a cat to the bowl of milk and create a very slick abstract composition: cat, tongue, milk."

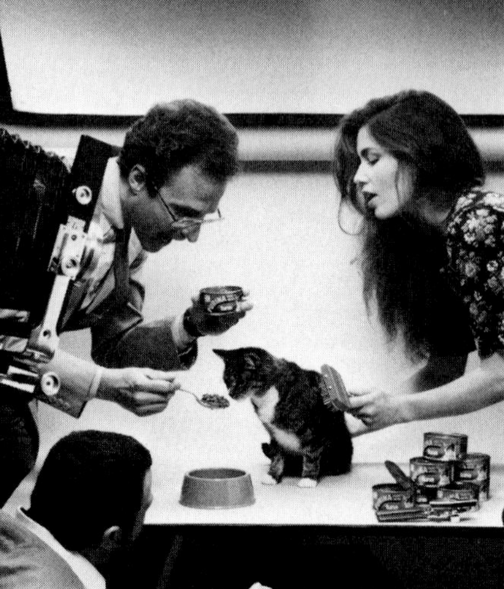

Ed Centner
New York
1980
How to shoot a cat ad: "We tried several trained cats, but they were too passive, and it wasn't interesting. Finally, a friend brought Maggie to the studio. She was stubborn, impatient and angry, but the pictures were great."

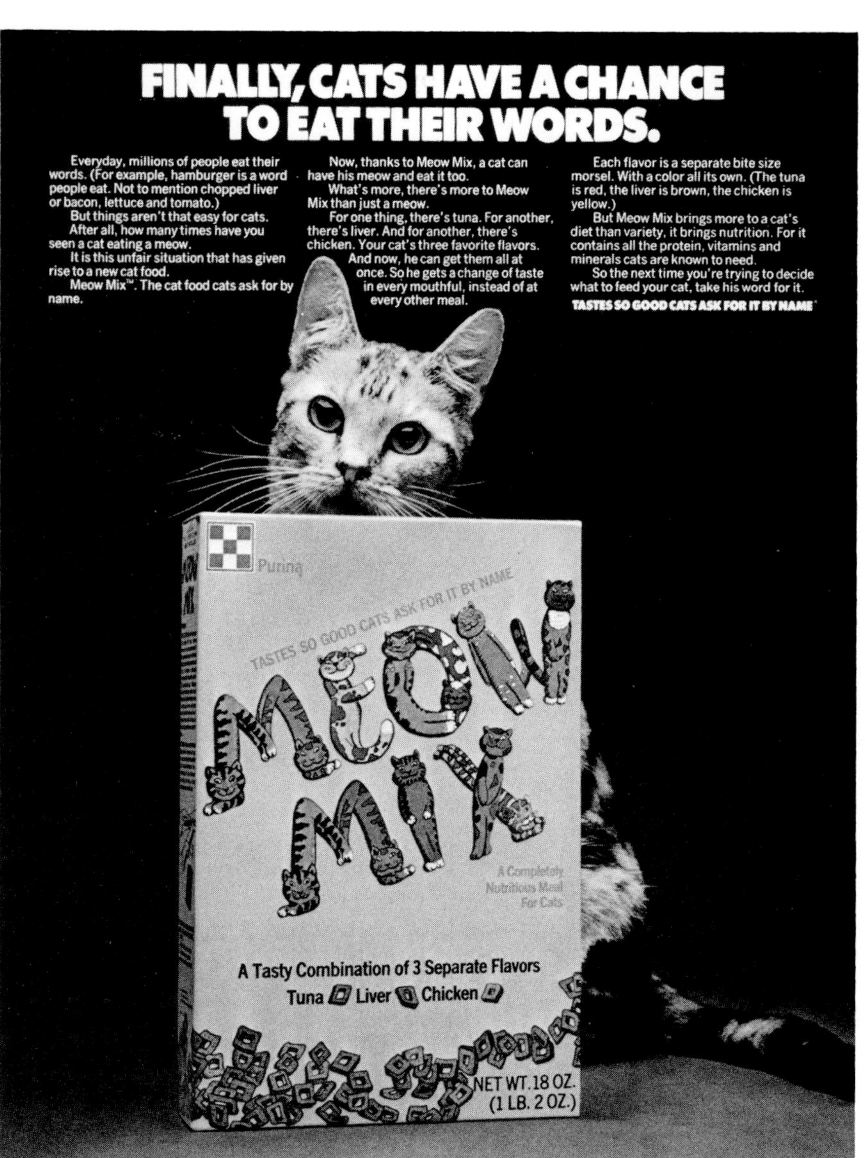

FINALLY, CATS HAVE A CHANCE TO EAT THEIR WORDS.
Everyday, millions of people eat their words. (For example, hamburger is a word people eat. Not to mention chopped liver or bacon, lettuce and tomato.)
But things aren't that easy for cats.
After all, how many times have you seen a cat eating a meow.
It is this unfair situation that has given rise to a new cat food.
Meow Mix™. The cat food cats ask for by name.
Now, thanks to Meow Mix, a cat can have his meow and eat it too.
What's more, there's more to Meow Mix than just a meow.
For one thing, there's tuna. For another, there's liver. And for another, there's chicken. Your cat's three favorite flavors.
And now, he can get them all at once. So he gets a change of taste in every mouthful, instead of at every other meal.
Each flavor is a separate bite size morsel. With a color all its own. (The tuna is red, the liver is brown, the chicken is yellow.)
But Meow Mix brings more to a cat's diet than variety, it brings nutrition. For it contains all the protein, vitamins and minerals cats are known to need.
So the next time you're trying to decide what to feed your cat, take his word for it.
TASTES SO GOOD CATS ASK FOR IT BY NAME
Purina
TASTES SO GOOD CATS ASK FOR IT BY NAME
MEOW MIX
A Tasty Combination of 3 Separate Flavors
Tuna Liver Chicken
NET WT. 18 OZ. (1 LB. 2 OZ.)

27

Della Famina,
Travisano
& Partners
advertisement for
Meow Mix
1979
The Ralston Purina Company's ads are slick and sophisticated. This one, by an award-winning agency, ran in several family magazines.

you out."

Another photographer told us, "A cat doesn't bother to try to con you. He's so cool he doesn't have to do anything to please you. Cats are so self-confident that they're completely unconcerned about what people—including photographers—think."

Some photographers sought out the editors of this book, from halfway around the world, to point out the importance of including their cat picture in this collection. The photograph of the descendants of Hemingway's cats in Florida is one of these. Sometimes the editors themselves spent weeks in search of a particular picture because its exclusion would be unthinkable. Bill Hayward's essay on fat cats, for example, would not be as meaningful without the picture of Tiger, the fattest cat in the world according to the BBC-TV show *Record Breakers* and the *Guinness Book of World Records*.

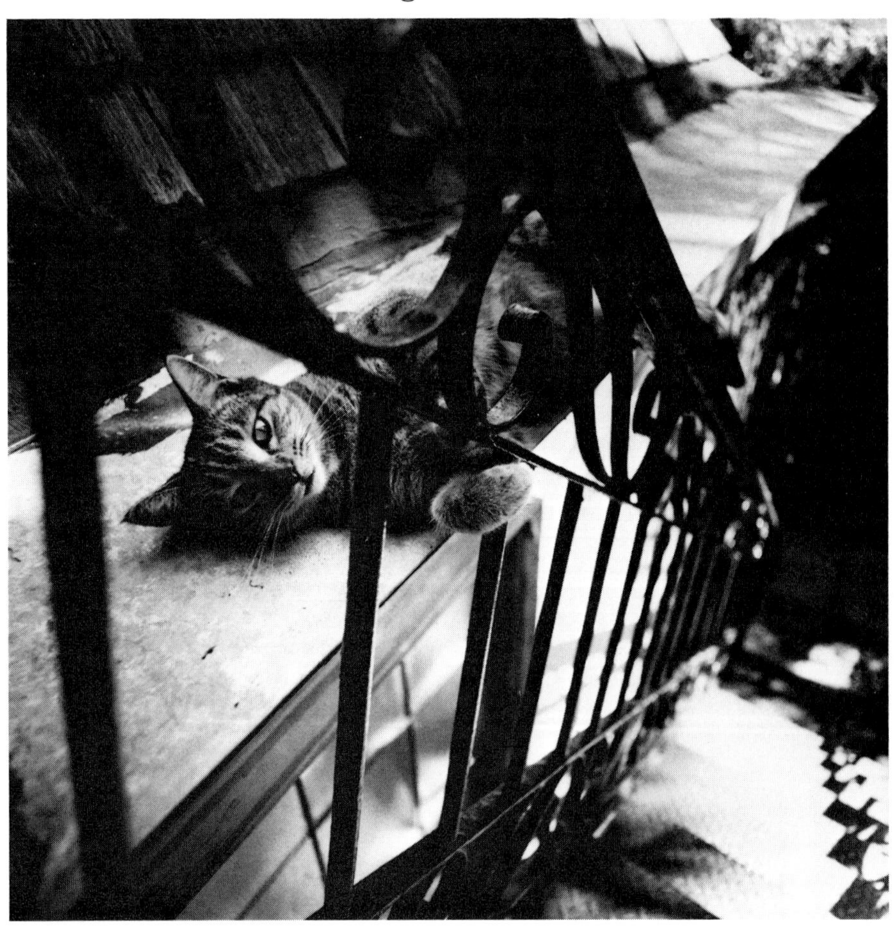

Arthur Tress
Key West
1979
A descendant of Ernest Hemingway's cats lounges around the famed author's former home in Florida.

Guinness Book of World Records
1979
Tiger, tipping the scales at 43 pounds, is presumed to be the world's fattest cat, according to the *Guiness Book of World Records*.
Shown here with Editor Norris McWhirter.

City Cats

Cats came to the city hundreds of years ago to keep people company and to kill rats. Today, very few still kill rats, but they've got other jobs. They hang around barber shops, butcher shops, train stations, antique shops, book stores, candy stores and delicatessens.

In short, they're still keeping people company.

City cats are tough and very stubborn. They've survived the worst winters living in alleyways and turning over garbage cans for dinner.

When you roam the streets in search of a photograph, city cats disappear, as if they were all part of a conspiracy. Great pictures of city cats only happen on *their* terms. They might show up at any time—either alone or in a pack—from under a parked car, or sitting at a window, or darting from one side of the street to the other.

Jill Freedman
Greenwich Village
1975
"I happened to notice this alley cat as I walked by. It was just all there."

André Kertesz
Paris
1928
"This is a very old cat—a typical concierge's cat. Everyone who passed the window would look and smile, but the cat would just stare back."

Ruth Orkin
1957
"I was walking down the steeet, and suddenly there was this white cat hanging out a black window. How could you not stop and shoot it, if you're a photographer?"

André Kertesz
Paris
1927
"I found this scene interesting. This is in the middle of Paris, on the Grand Boulevard."

Ruth Orkin
Women Feeding Cats
Rome
1951
"When I was in Rome, I was told that if an old ruin is discovered during construction, by law, they must preserve it.
Here's one I found by leaning through an opening in a modern building."

Philippe Salaün
Nimes
1976
"The poor cat got locked out of his home, a flower shop. I caught him trying to get people's attention inside. The poster, advertising a dog show, just added drama to the moment."

Facing Page:
Harvey Stein
Coney Island
1973
"I go to Coney Island quite a bit to photograph. That day I was photographing people, and I saw this cat sitting on a stool in an open-air bar."

Following Pages:
Henri Cartier-Bresson
Shop Window
Lille Nord, France
1968

André Kertesz
Paris
1928
"If there's a situation I like, I'll take it. I especially liked this. You can find this only in Paris."

Kittens

The trouble with a kitten is
THAT
Eventually it becomes a
CAT

Ogden Nash
The Kitten

The photographs on the following pages reveal that photographers universally find kittens appealing. Most of the great photographs of kittens, like almost all the photographs in this book, are spontaneous and unplanned. Witness Rick Smolan's photograph of a kitten, taken while on assignment for *Time* Magazine, when he was covering blacks in the South. And Jill Freedman's "cat on a leash" was shot while walking through New York's Washington Square Park on *her* way to an assignment.

Even the most world-weary and cynical among us (excluding perhaps Ogden Nash) is vulnerable to the innocence and beguilement of newborn kittens.

Yet, as most owners know, a cat is only a kitten for a poignant, but relatively brief, period of time. In fact, the first twenty-one days of a kitten's existence are roughly equivalent to the first year and a half of an infant's life.

Eleni Mylonos
Troglodyte
England
1974
"He was a man in the countryside near Schenley, England, living in a very rundown shack in a field in the middle of nowhere. He was once a gardener. All he had was this family of cats. He seemed to be posing with the kittens, as if they were his prized possessions."

Jill Freedman
London
1969
"A friend's cat had newborn kittens. You can see the tail of the mother in this photograph."

Jill Freedman
Washington Square Park
1978
"This guy was trying to teach his kitten to walk outside, on a leash. The cat obviously did not want to be out. I think it's a very funny picture."

Brian Lav
Tony's Kitten
Elizabeth, New Jersey
1979

Rick Smolan
Elkins, South Carolina
1975
"I was doing a story on blacks in America, for *Time*. This cat was crawling up the screen door of the house of a very, very poor black family, with whom I'd spent a few days. Since I often carry a Leica that I use for doing my own pictures while I'm on assignment, I just fired off a few frames. I don't watch cats, specifically, but if I see one doing something interesting, I'll take some pictures."

Jim Bengston
Norway
1978

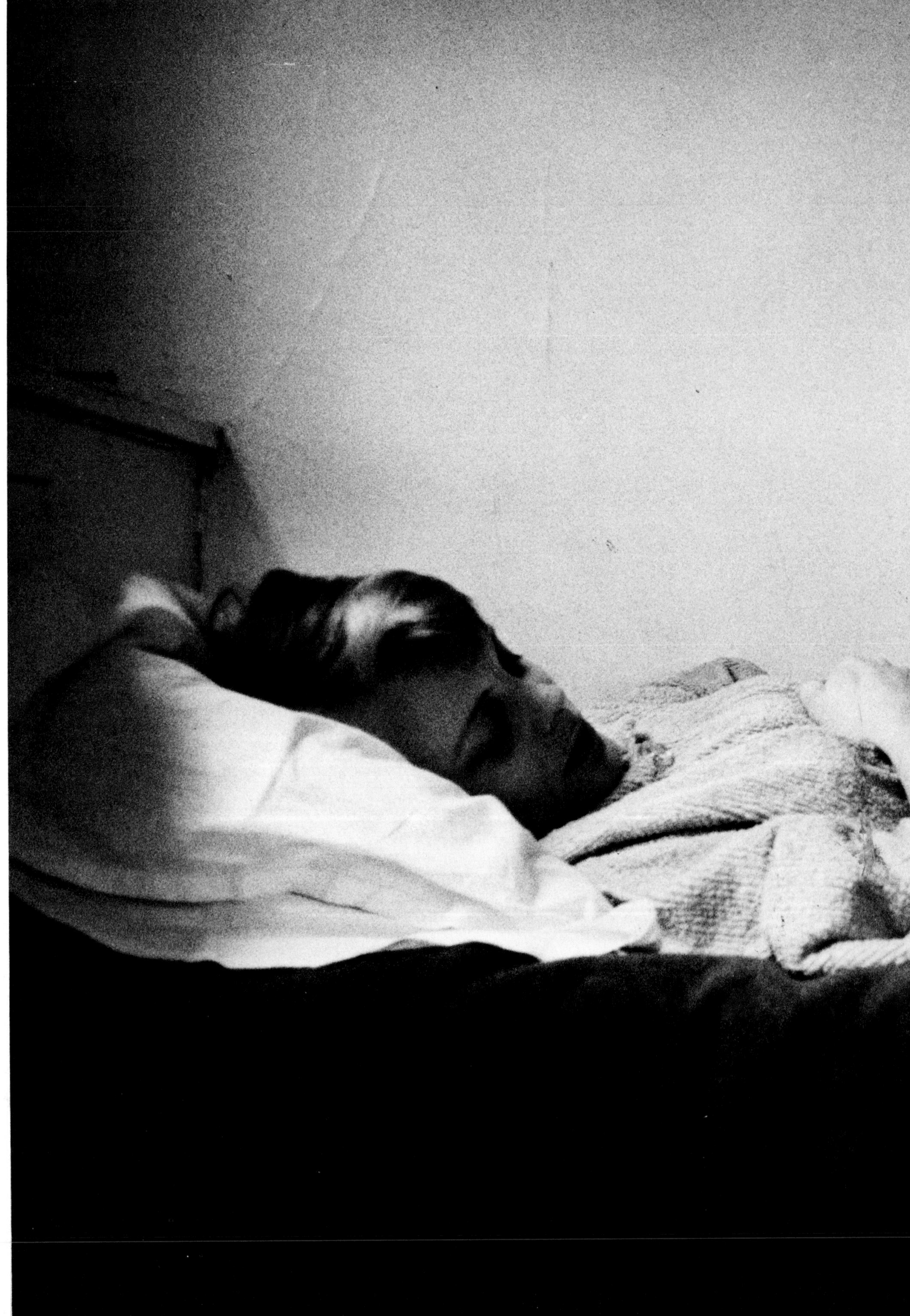

Previous Pages:
Elliot Erwitt
Louie
New York
1952

Above:
Jane Schreibman
Venice
1979
"Photographing cats gives me an opportunity to work with light and movement, without having to deal with people.
I took this on the island of Buranos, near Venice."

Jane Schreibman
Venice
1979
"This little kitten had been abandoned by its parents, so I took it home and cleaned it up. I photographed it asleep in the chair, just moving it to different spots to catch the light."

Of Cats and Kids

I like little Pussy, her coat is so warm And if I don't hurt her she'll do me no harm; So I'll not pull her tail, nor drive her away But Pussy and I very gently will play.

Nursery Rhyme, Anonymous
Kitty; How to Treat Her

The gentle relationship between children and cats seems to intrigue photographers, as much as it does our poets and writers. This intimacy between the two is sharply defined in the photographs that follow.

Diane Marino's wonderful picture of a young girl, literally twisting a cat's head towards the camera, perhaps evokes most lyrically this essential trust between cats and children.

Most of our photographers pointed out to us that photographing cats is like photographing children. You can't force them to pose—they get bored easily—but when you get a great shot, it's worth the waiting.

William Coupon
New York
1980
"Bianca is a kid who lives in my building. She's real precocious and a terrific model. This is her own cat, who catches mice in her family's country home. I told her to do just what she wanted with her cat, and the cat was semi-tolerable during all of this.
At first, I wanted to do her nude with the cat, but it would have been a problem, with the cat's scratching."

Eleni Mylonos
Athens, Greece
1976
"I found this little kitten in my mother's backyard, and my brother and I adopted him. As soon as I lifted up my camera, my niece, Christina, put the cat in front of her face."

Diane Marino
Malverne, Long Island
1978
"The little girl, Valery, lived in the neighborhood, and used to come over and talk to my sister and me. The reason she's holding Taba this way is because Taba wasn't looking at the camera. So she grabbed its head and pointed it. I used to call this photograph, 'Don't worry, the cat's alright.'"

Jill Krementz
New York
1977
Nancy Menapace, and her cat, on a peaceful afternoon.

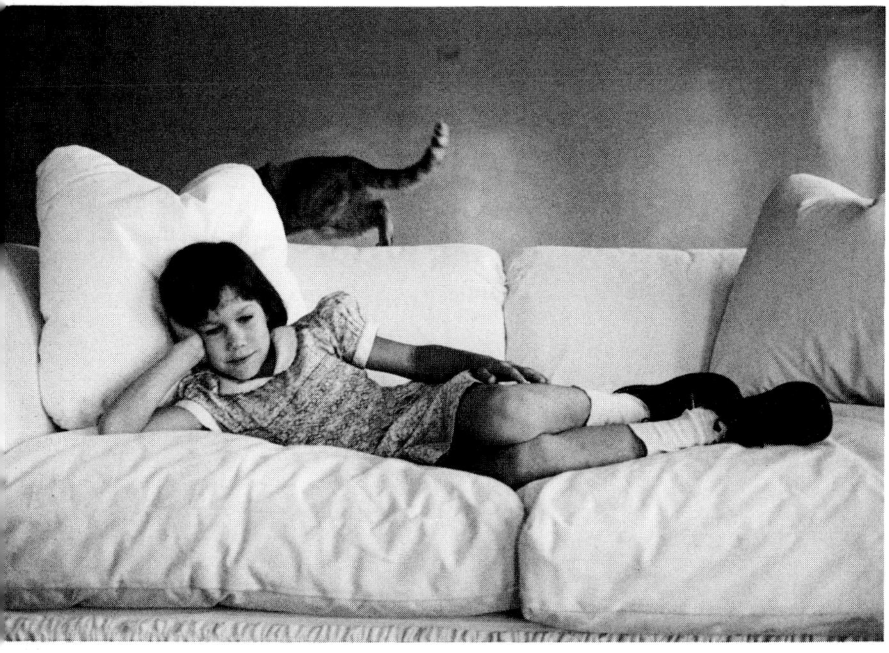

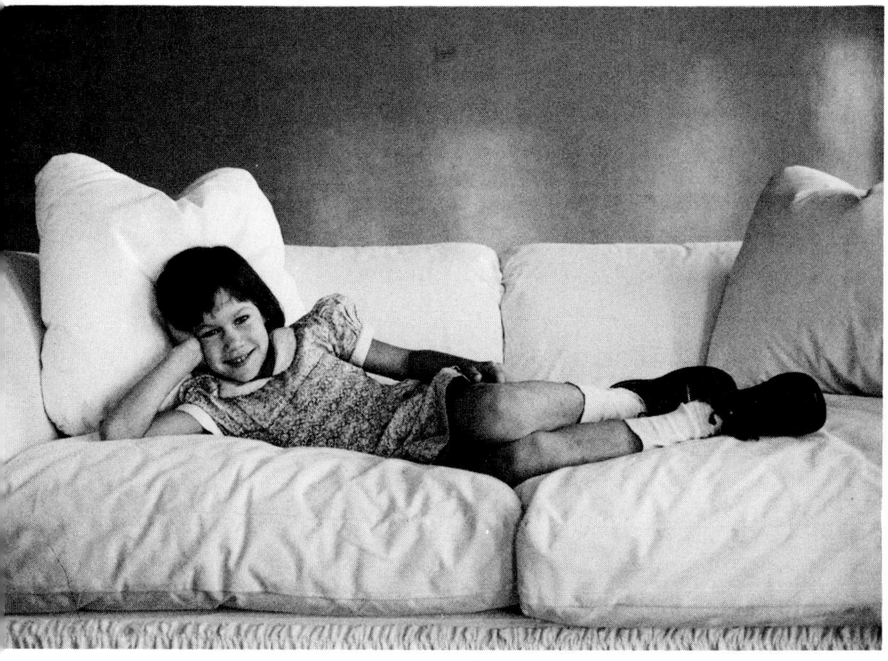

Duane Michals
Margaret Finds A Box
Newark, New Jersey
1970
"I always try to stick a cat in a picture, but the problem is you simply *don't* tell cats what to do.
This was an idea from my childhood: As soon as a refrigerator or washing machine would arrive in a huge cardboard box, the kids would climb into it, and turn it into a fort or an airplane or tunnel or whatever.
This little girl finds a box in her living room, and gets into it, and flies away.
I feel there is something about cats and children that adds a fairy-tale feeling to photographs."

The Family of Cats

There are over forty-five million cats in the United States, and they infiltrate the entire spectrum of our society. You will find cats with derelicts in back alleys and with dowagers in Palm Beach. They are loyal and true companions, and discrimination, for any reason, is not part of their raison d'être.

The Family of Cats are shown fulfilling their roles as companions and compatriots to people in all walks of life—from David Seymour's photographs of a bishop in Greece, to Jill Freedman's candid shot of a young man on the beach at Fire Island.

Photographer Unknown
1890's
Woman with cat. From a glass negative.

David Seymour
Greece
1954
A Mateora Monastery monk is greeted by his young cat, who has appeared at the window of his room early in the morning.

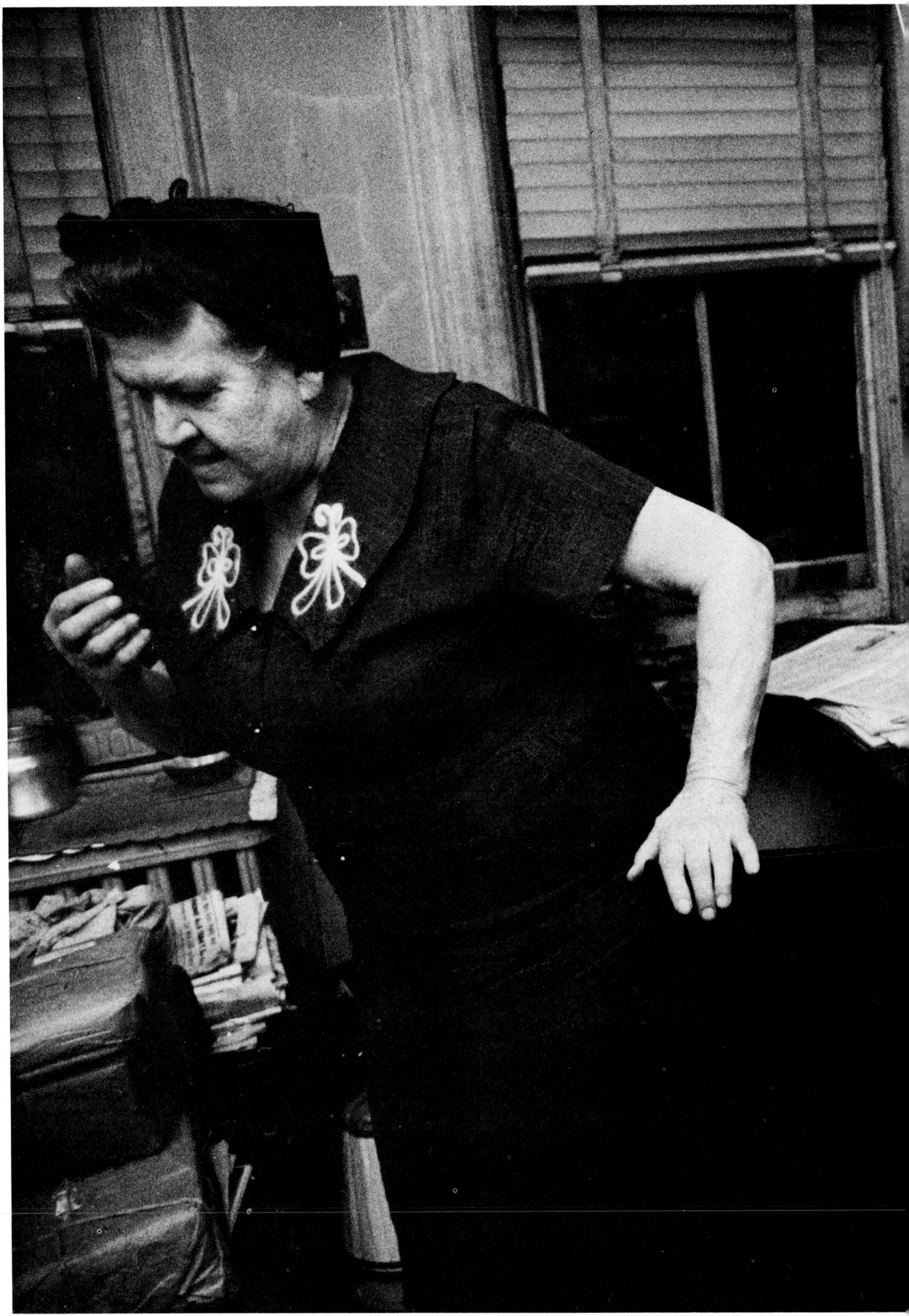

Previous pages:
Bruce Davidson
Woman and Cat
New York City
1958

Above:
Suzanne Opton
Chelsea, Vermont
1974
"This is Edith Mason's prized cat. She loved this photograph so much that she used it for her Christmas cards. She and her husband have about eighteen cats—separated according to their sex so they don't breed."

Jill Freedman
Fire Island
1974
"I was walking on the beach when I took this shot. I have no idea who the man is, but I love it."

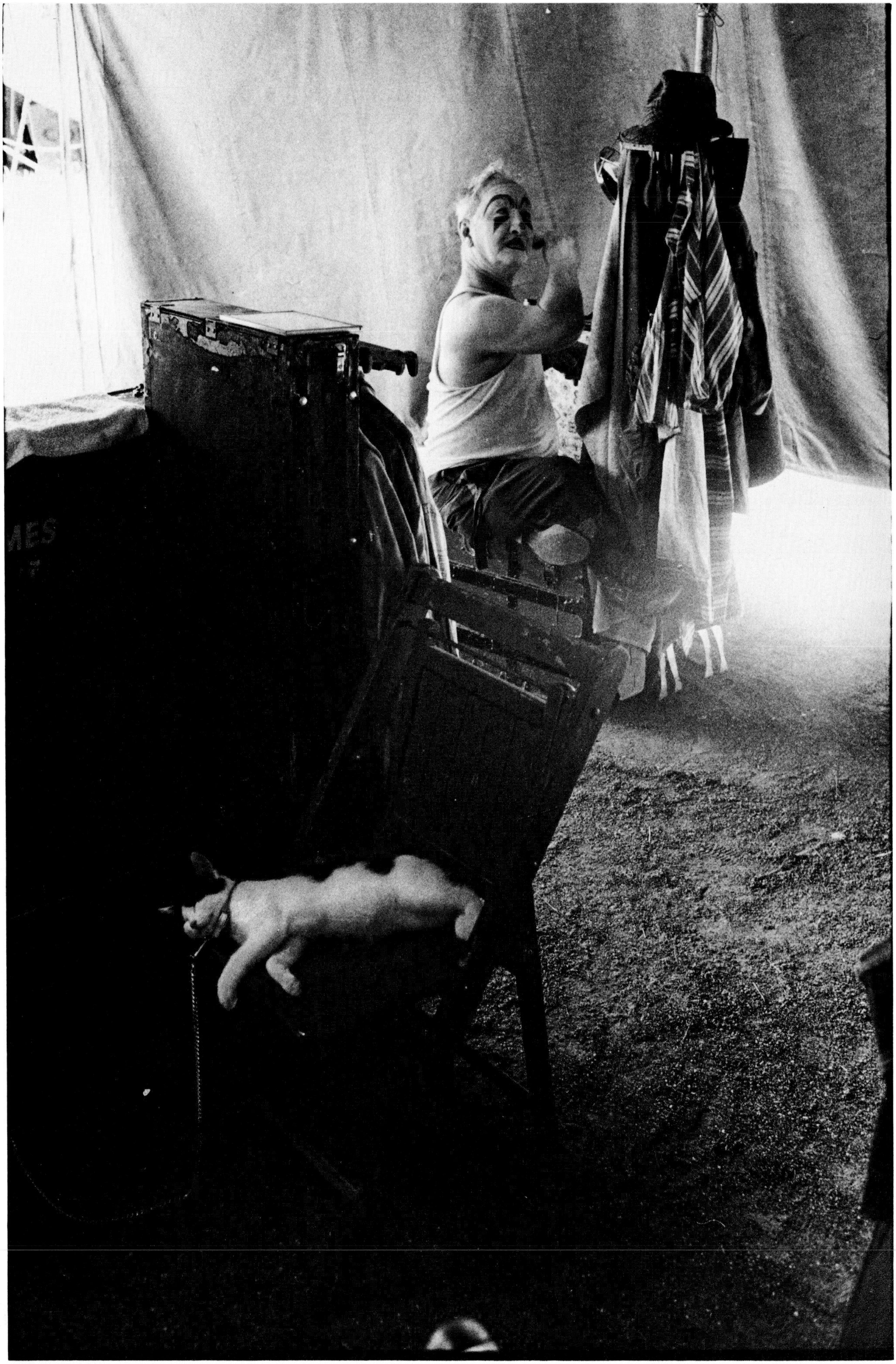

Previous pages:
Jill Freedman
Gladys and Shorty
1971
"This is from my book, *Circus Days*. Gladys belonged to Shorty, one of the clowns, and is chained so she won't run away. That's Shorty in the background, making up."

Terry Gruber
Paramus, New Jersey
1979
"This seemed to me like the perfect combination: It was taken at a cat show in Paramus."

Above:
Barbara Alper
Staten Island
1980
"When a cat trusts people, he'll turn over and present his stomach."

Antonio Mendoza
New York City
1980
"Ernie is in the arms of his owner, Nancy Frank. He's usually aware of the camera for a while before he gets bored, because he knows that the camera represents something that I do to him. Yet, he can't quite figure it out."

The Cat Who Walks Alone

When cats reach the age of five months, they're no longer kittens; they are now considered young adults, ready to face the world on their own. Even though, as littermates, they enjoyed each other's warmth and companionship, at one year they have no memory of their parents or siblings.

They now assume an independence and solitude not found among most animals. Unlike dogs or sheep, they have no sense of the pack or herd. Yet, interestingly enough, when forced together as a group, they seem to adapt more readily than dogs.

The faces of these cats—whether curious, bored, bemused or seductive—reflect self-assurance and a sense of independence.

Brian Lav
George's Cat
Iselin, New Jersey
1979

Photographer Unknown
1890's
This print is from a recently discovered glass plate. Photography took a new turn in the 1870's when factories began to mass produce gelatin silver bromide emulsion for glass plates. These "dry plates" were more sensitive than wet plates and didn't have to be developed immediately.

Steichen
The Cat
1902
Unsigned platinum print.

Susan Chang
Irvington, New York
1975
"I was staying with friends in the country and their Angora cat, Scarlet, reminded me of my cat, who was waiting for me in California. She really blended into the outdoors."

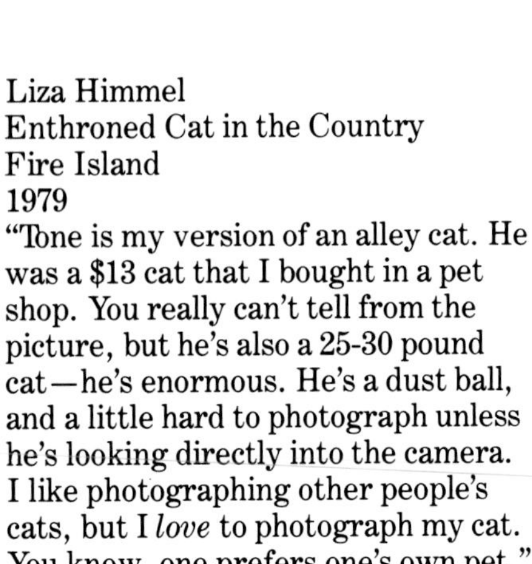

Liza Himmel
Enthroned Cat in the Country
Fire Island
1979
"Tone is my version of an alley cat. He was a $13 cat that I bought in a pet shop. You really can't tell from the picture, but he's also a 25-30 pound cat—he's enormous. He's a dust ball, and a little hard to photograph unless he's looking directly into the camera. I like photographing other people's cats, but I *love* to photograph my cat. You know, one prefers one's own pet."

Matthew Klein
Armstrong
New York
1971
"Armstrong is one of my oldest friends. He's now ten years old. This picture was taken after I had had a very interesting encounter with him. I was sitting around reading a book, when I sensed that he was looking at me. When I turned around and confronted him he adjusted his glare about fifteen degrees. This went on a few more times... sometimes I'd catch him looking, and he'd look away; sometimes I'd stare at him, and he'd catch me, and *I'd* look away in turn. I realized that Armstrong was a serious being to contend with. It also changed my way of seeing forever."

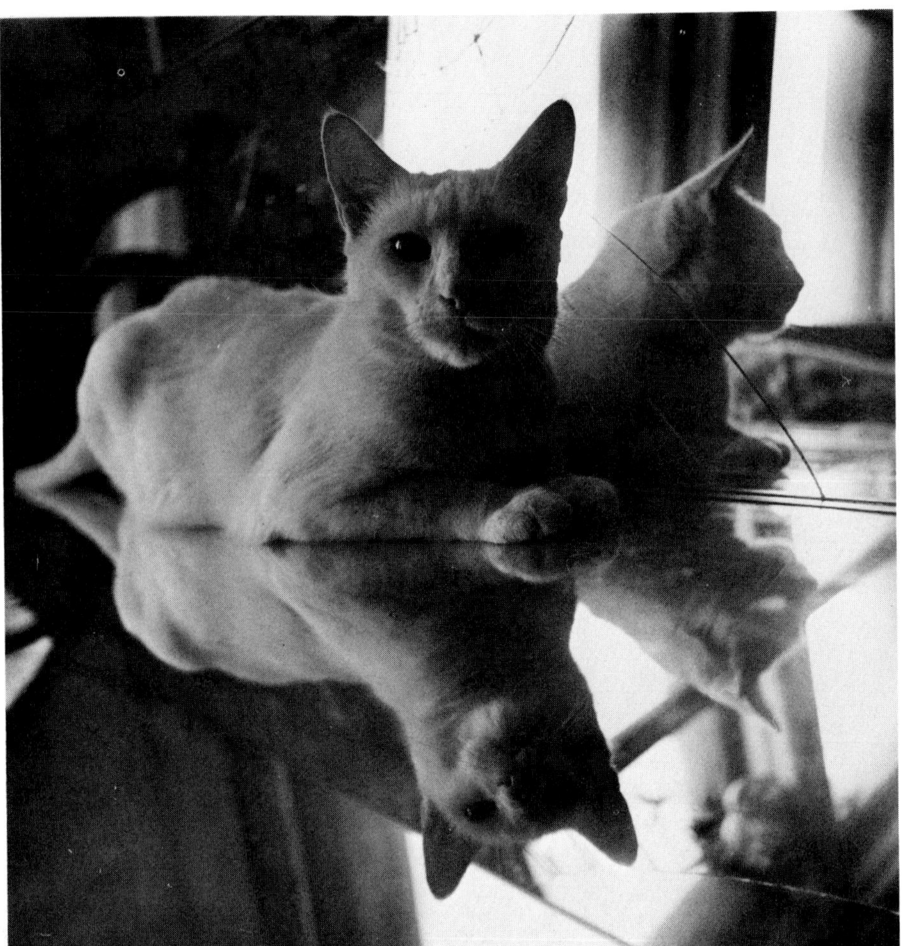

Arthur Tress
New York
1978
A mysterious-looking white cat rests on his reflection.

George Tice
Iselin, New Jersey
From the *Cat Series*
1978
"I like the way white cats glow in the woods. I've been doing a series on cats, photographing them in the woods across from my house. Following them allows you to become very aware of their abilities—as hunters—how much they see, their awareness, their caution. At every step they turn, and look about, to see if there are any predators."

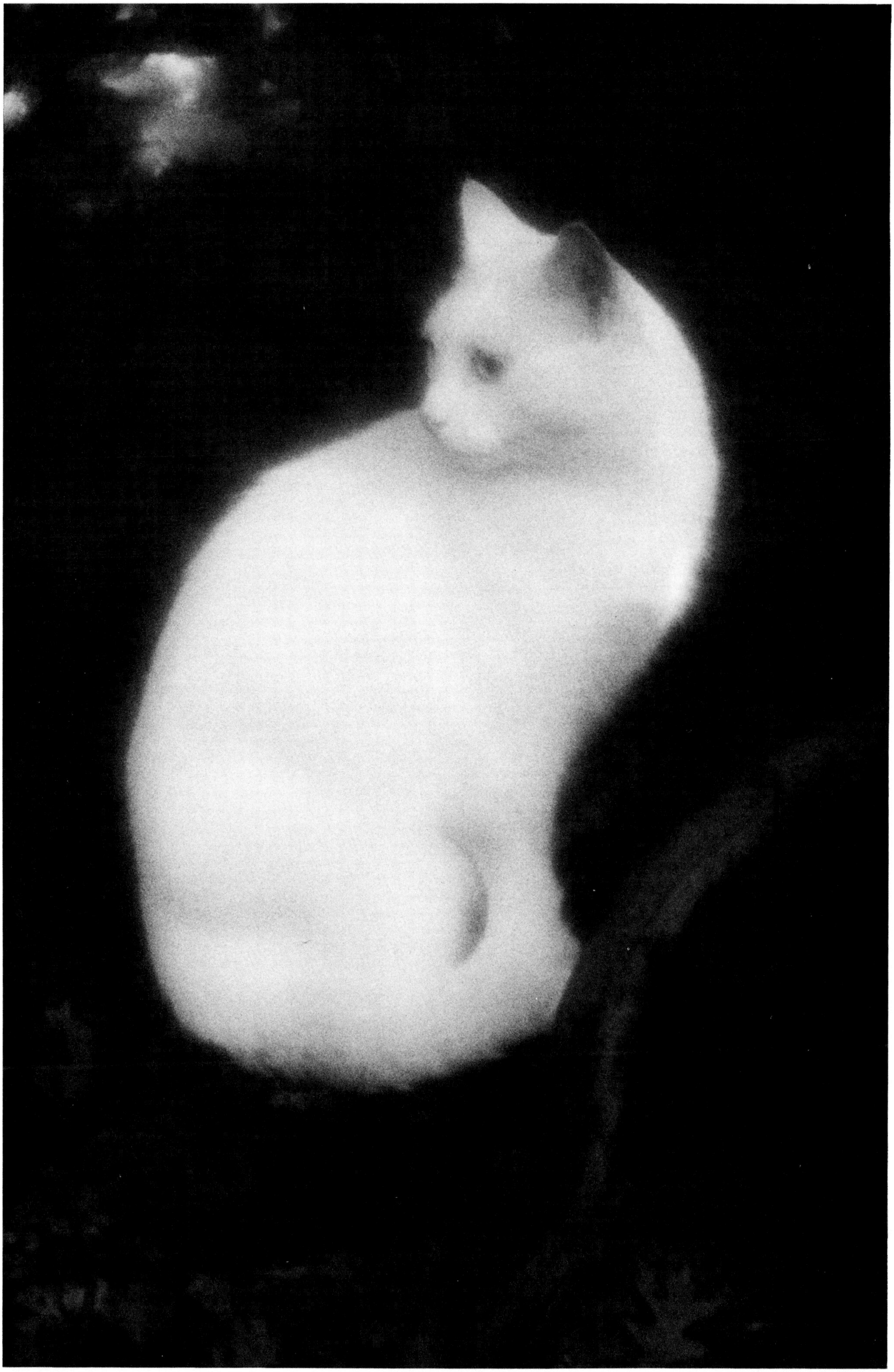

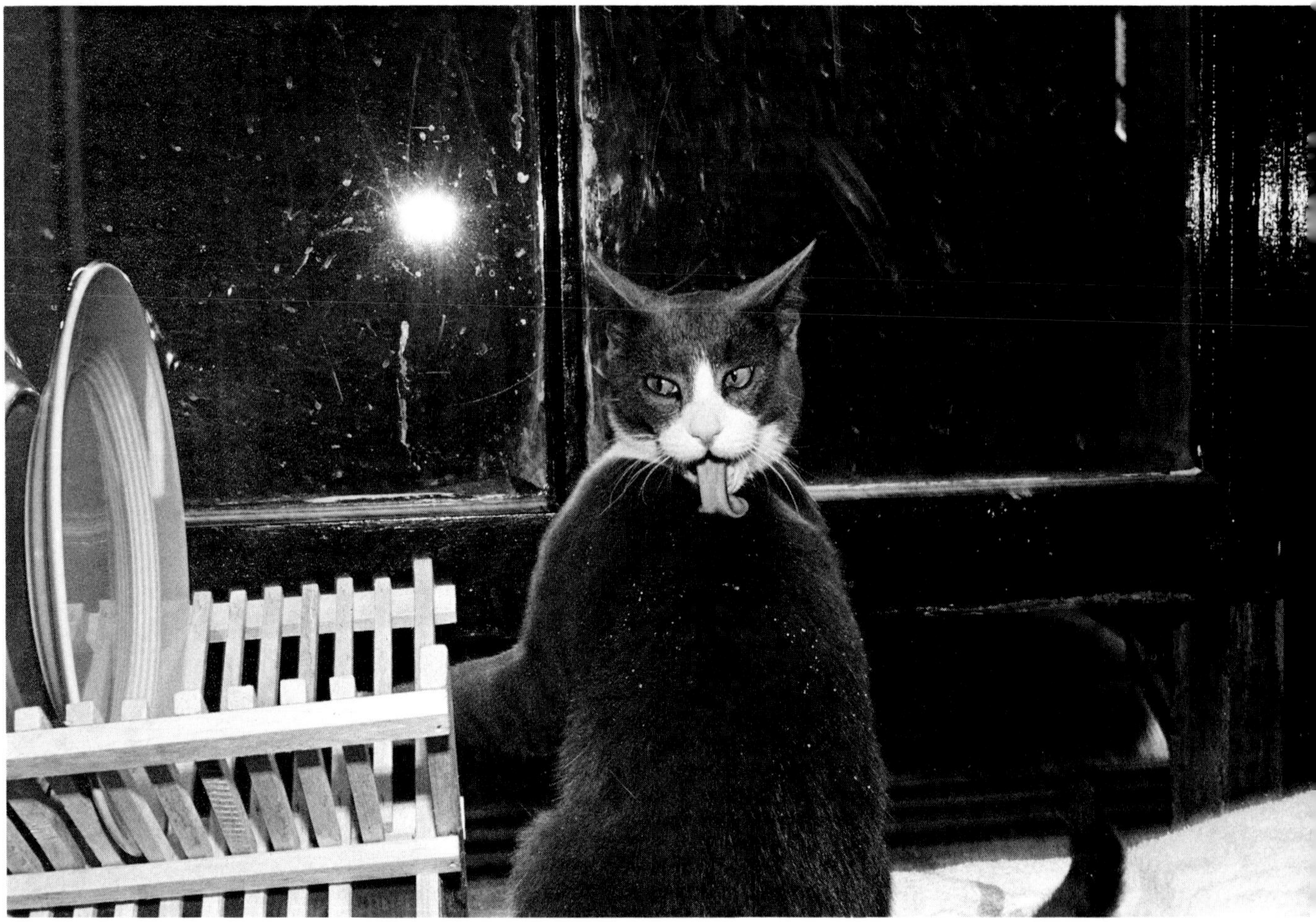

Antonio Mendoza
New York City
1980
"I'm amazed by how flexible cats are. They can move their bodies with such ease into virtually any position. I thought that this was a very typical moment—Ernie turning his head 180 degrees.
"Like most cats, he spends a lot of time cleaning himself."

Jill Freedman
Cat Taking a Nap on a Pile of Coats in a Gallery.
New York
1976

Dan Wynn
New York
1970
"I first tried this down in my studio, but it wouldn't work, because Licorice, our kitten, was only familiar with our living quarters upstairs. I brought some white paper upstairs, because I just wanted to silhouette him, and we started playing some games. All of a sudden he turned around and looked at me and bam! I took it."

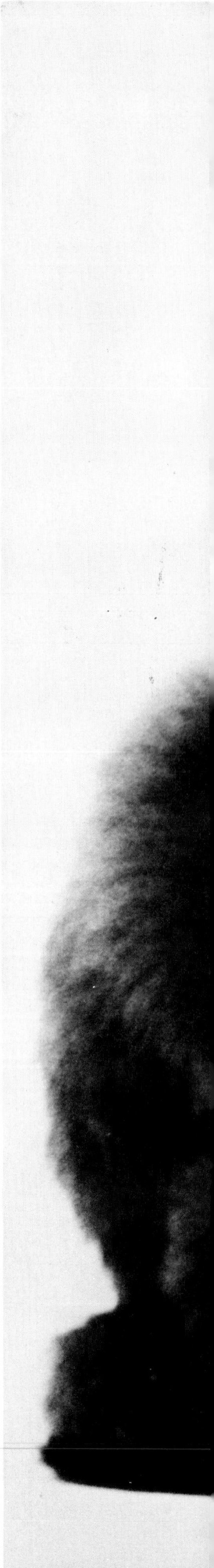

Armen Katchaturian
New York City
1980
"I approached photographing Max the way I approach photographing people, that is, direct contact with the camera became direct contact with the viewer. I don't have a cat. I just spread my love around to other people's animals, and it satisfies me that way."

Anthony Lowe
Studio, New York City
1979
"No matter where I'm working, that' where Geoffrey Adam Hotus wants t be.
I had just started shooting, and he literally jumped into the picture. Instead of telling him to 'shoo,' I just looked through the camera and shot off 36 pictures."

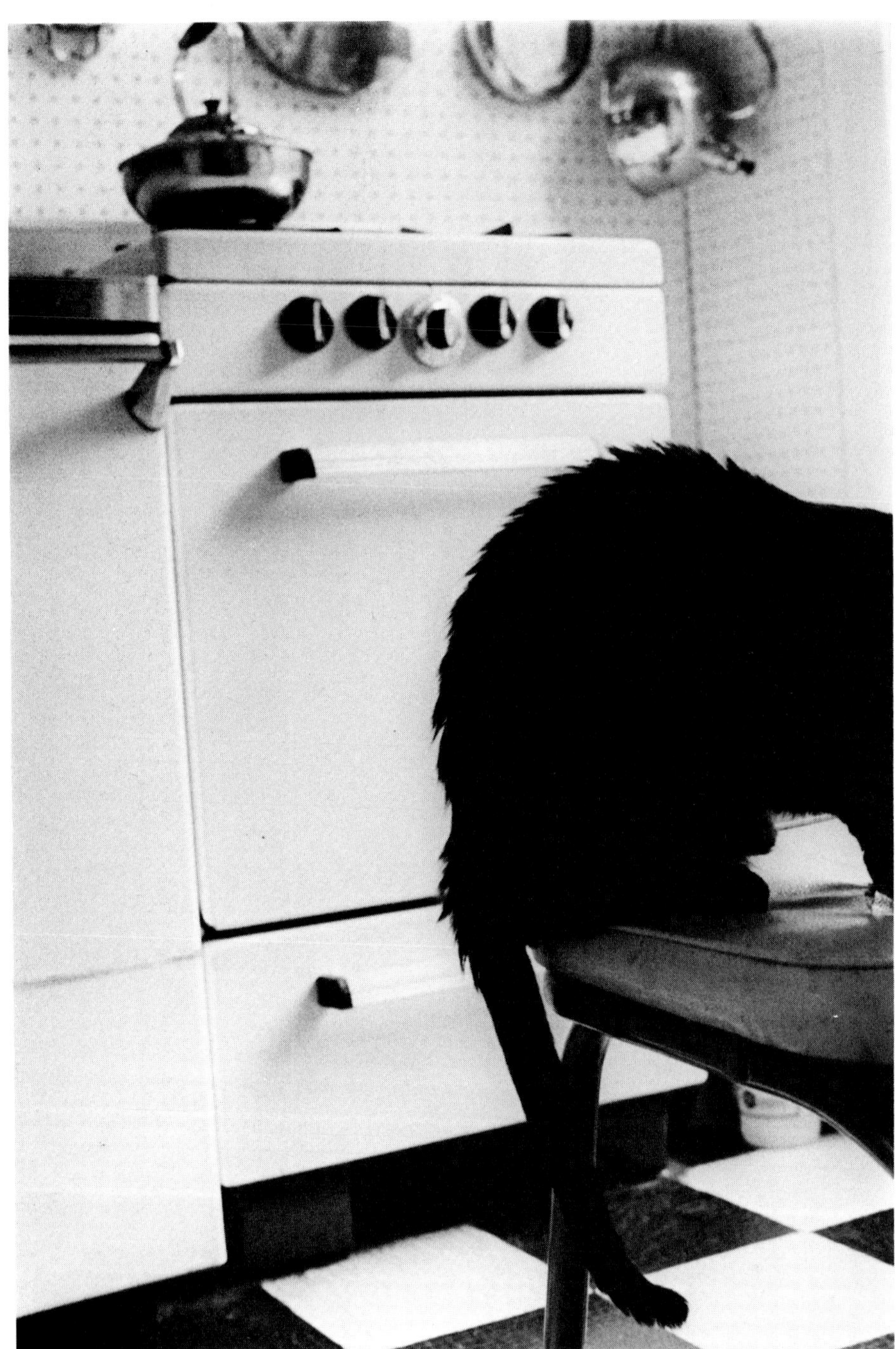

Carol Weinberg
Black and White
New York
1976
"The best way to shoot cats is to follow them and watch what they do, or give them something they haven't seen before. I was following my two cats around that day and using them as a design factor."

Lawrence Robbins
Conway, Massachusetts
1977

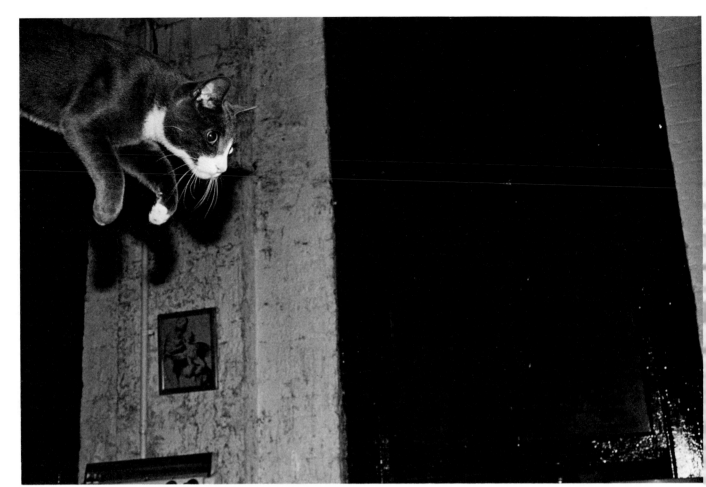

Antonio Mendoza
New York
1979
"Cats suddenly find themselves in high places, and, when you think that there is no way down for them, they leap at their objective with grace and precision."

Jean C. Pigozzi
Paris
1977
"I don't particularly like cats—I despise dogs, however—but I always find myself photographing them."

Cats and Other Strangers

The cat—for the most part—keeps her distance from other animals just as she does with her own species. The kitten, of course, is an exception.

In Jane Schreibman's photograph (page 96), a young kitten is unsuccessfully trying to suckle an extremely tolerant and amiable dog. More typical is Jill Freedman's shot of a cat in a tree, regally and confidently avoiding a dog in swift pursuit, (page 93).

Peter Kaplan's cream blue Persian (page 98) who has successfully captured a mouse, is portrayed as aggressor, while Barbara Morgan's Toad-Kitten (page 99) again illustrates the trusting nature of a kitten.

But perhaps the essence of a cat's true personality is curiosity, tempered by a measured degree of caution, best illustrated by Carol Weinberg's photograph below.

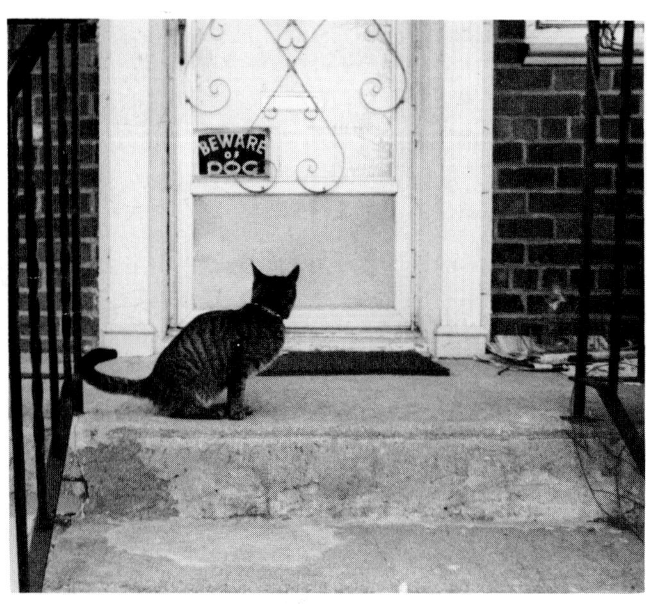

Carol Weinberg
But Can the Cat Read?
Bayside, New York
1964

Jill Freedman
Connecticut
1973
"It's one of my favorites. Lewis, the dog, and Smoke belong to two friends in Connecticut. Lewis and Smoke are basically friends—sometimes they get along, and sometimes they don't."

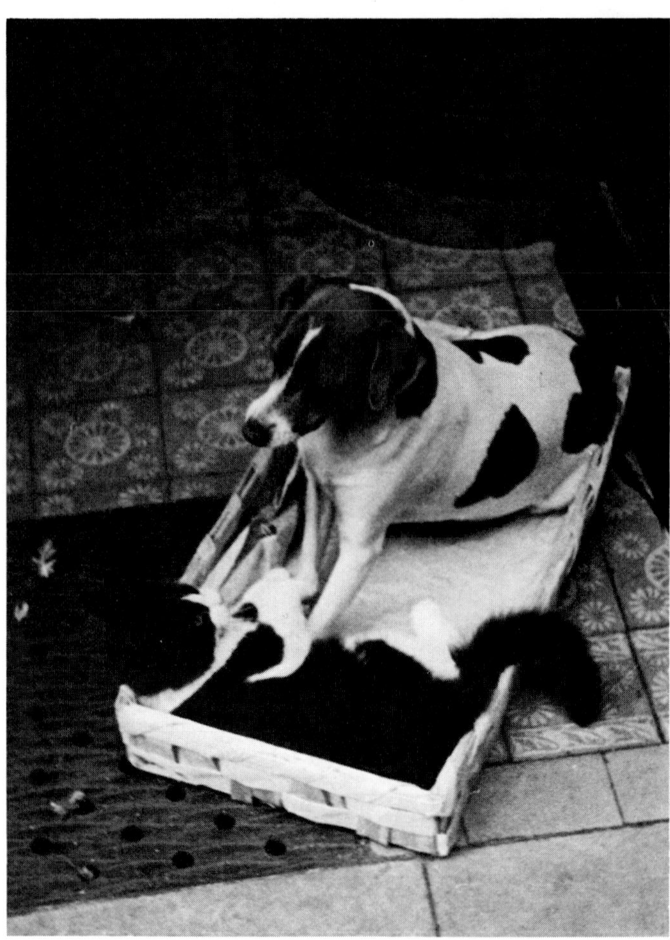

André Kertesz
Paris
1928
"This was in the entrance to a meat shop in Paris."

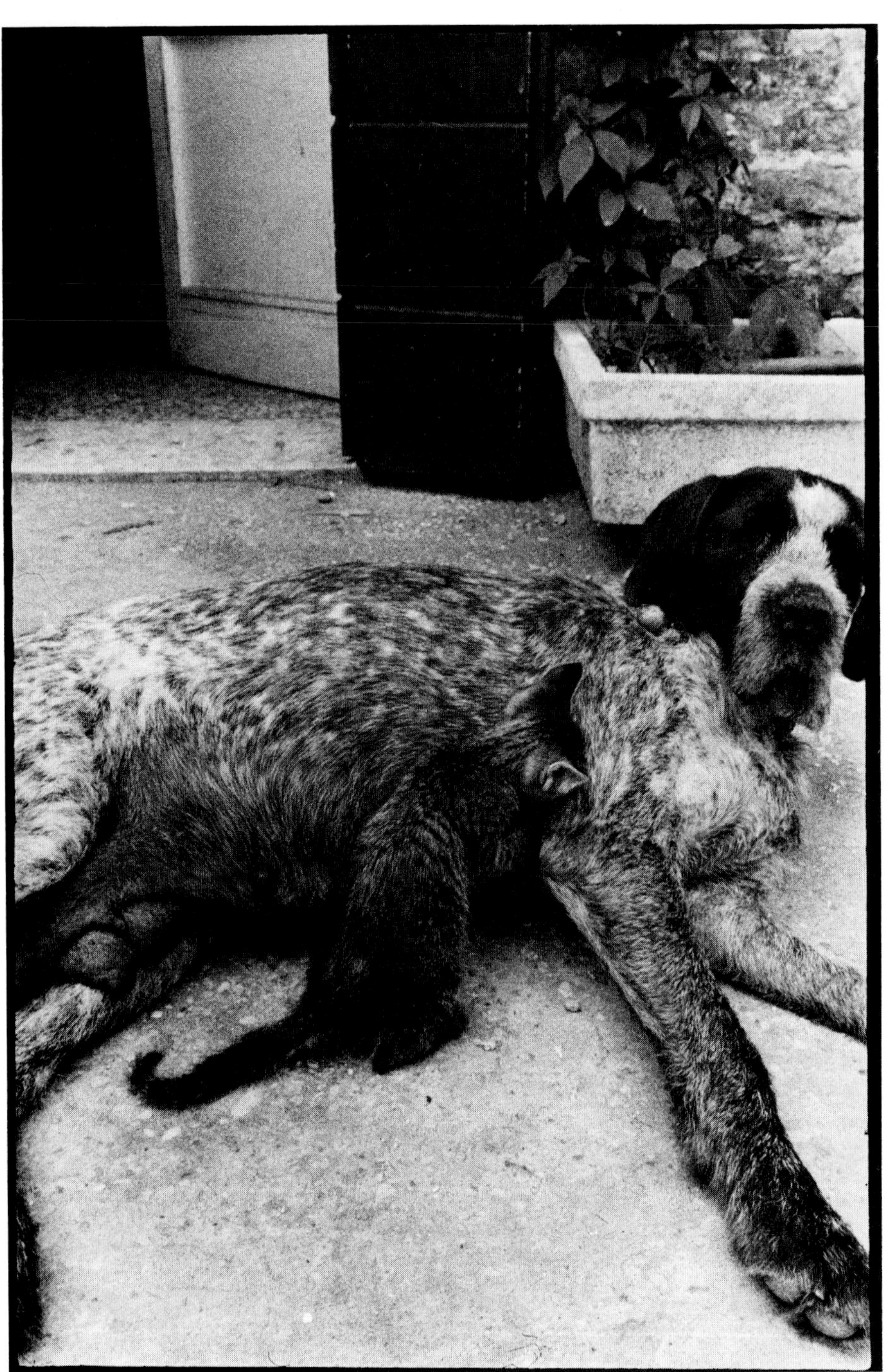

Jane Schreibman
Venice
1979
"This is an abandoned kitten that I had taken home. He obviously didn't know better and was trying to nurse from our neighbor's dog, which the dog blithely ignored."

Photographer Unknown
1920's
This healthy young kitten appears to be thriving on cow's milk. In fact, cat's milk is 10 percent protein, as opposed to cow's milk, which is only 3.2 percent protein.

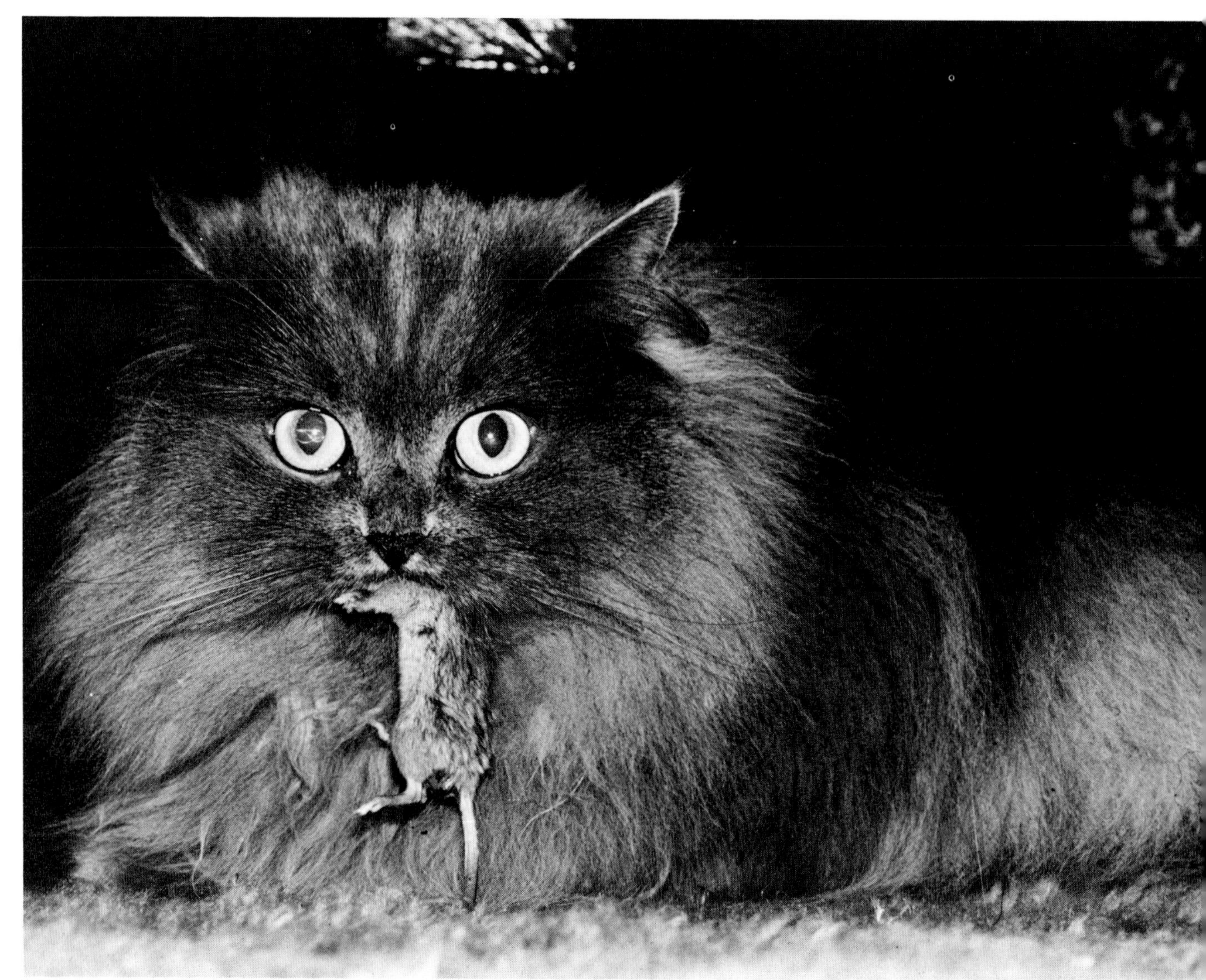

Peter B. Kaplan
New York
1978
"This was taken on my birthday. It was Tristanna's gift to me, I presume. She'd been watching one spot for a couple of days. All of a sudden the mouse made a dumb move, and the cat made the right one. She's an incredibly quick mouser."

Barbara Morgan
Doug and Toad-Kitten.
Scarsdale, New York
1942
"The cat is contemplating, and the toad is meditating.
"My son, Doug, was very fond of his kitten, and the kitten trusted him completely. He had just found this toad and discovered that the kitten would tolerate the toad. He burst into my studio to tell me about his discovery of a new animal—a toad-kitten."

Above:
Antonio Mendoza
New York City
New Year's Eve, 1979
"The cat on the left is Ernie, who lives with me in my loft. The other cat was found on the street, and was recognized as the neighborhood-butcher's cat, so we took him in for the weekend. Ernie was quite intrigued, because it was his first encounter with another fellow of his species. They looked at each other from quite a distance all night long. I crawled on the floor with my camera and started stalking them. After about 30 minutes (I have a lot of patience), Ernie became bold, and I took these two photographs. They immediately separated and hid from each other for the rest of the evening."

Previous pages:
Carl Fisher
New York
1970
"I did this in my studio. First I shot a cat on a trash can, and then I double-printed it. It makes a nice design.

Following Page:
Leonard Freed
Naples
1958

Previous page:
Guy Le Querrec
Suburb near Paris
1976

Above:
Rick Smolan
Carlyle, Pennsylvania
1970
"I shot Peas and Carrots on Thanksgiving Eve—I liked the way they slept together."

Eleni Mylonos
Syros, Greece
1978
"I like being around cats. I think it would be difficult to set them up and photograph them, if one had something specific in mind. I would feel I was manipulating them.
This is a brother and sister who were born in my mother's backyard in Athens. They played together, slept together, and lay together."

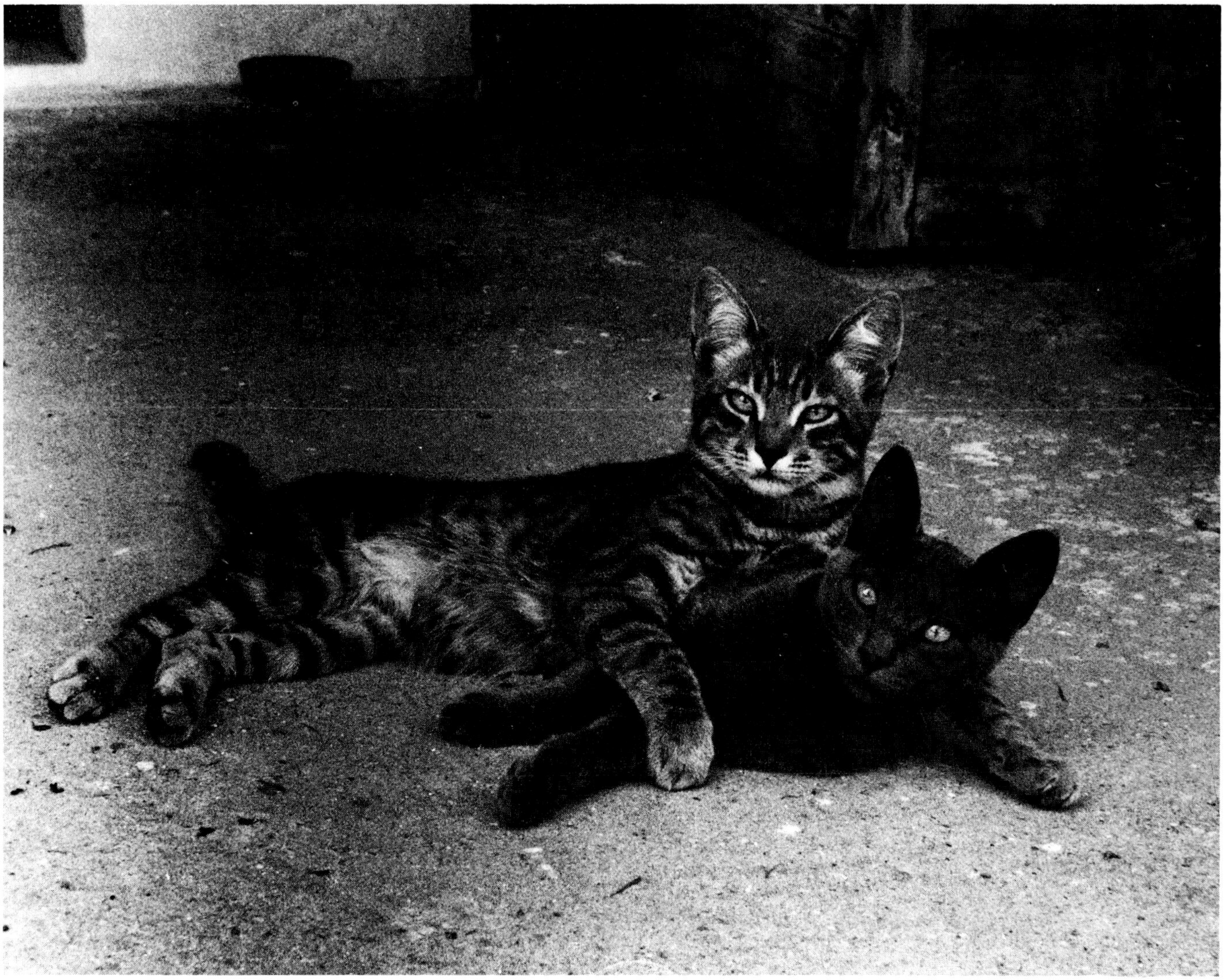

Cultured Cats

The cat has been a constant companion to artists and writers since the beginning of the sixteenth century. Writers, especially, must go through periods of intense concentration without much contact with others. Yet you'll find many of them sharing their abode with cats—cats that, though sharing their presence, make no demands of them.

The sixteenth century writer, Joachim du Bellay, was one of the first poets to eulogize his own cat, Belaud, in a poem shortly after Belaud died. And two hundred years later, Samuel Johnson, a fervent, if somewhat fanatical, devotee of cats, ordered his beloved cat, Hodge, to be fed only a diet of oysters when it began to show signs of aging.

The photographs that follow illustrate that this special kinship between felines and artists has not diminished with the years, and seems to be on the increase.

Hemingway, whether in Paris, Key West, or Ketcham, loved being surrounded by his many cats. And Colette probably summed up most artists and writers affection for cats with her marvelous observation: "Our perfect companions never have fewer than four feet."

Photographer Unknown
Picasso in His Studio
Paris
1910?
A young Pablo Picasso during the Cubist period with his Siamese cat. According to the diaries of Fernande Olivier, the woman who shared his life then, Picasso had two cats, a dog, and a monkey.

Jill Krementz
New York
1976
Writer Edward Gorey with some of his cats.

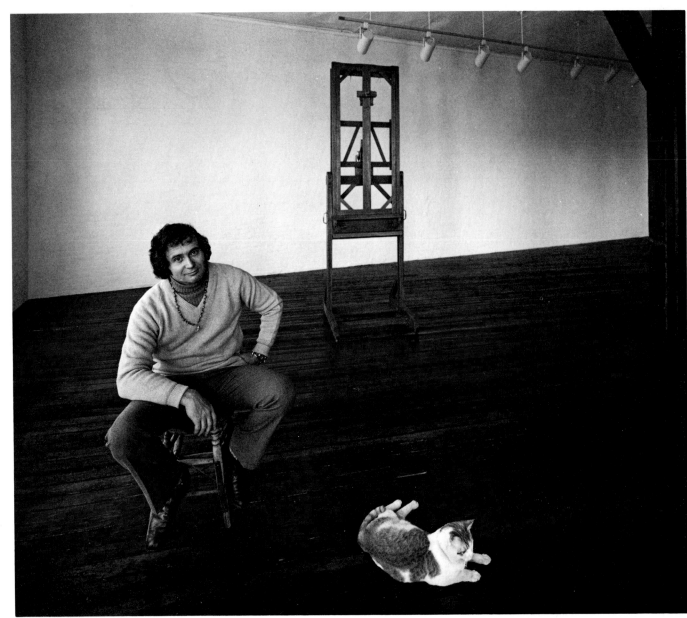

Arnold Newman
Robert Indiana's Studio, New York
1971
"I was doing a portrait of Indiana and I allowed the serendipity to take over. Indiana's cat turned out to be perfect."

Philippe Halsman
New York
1961
"Edward Albee loved cats. He brought his own cat and put him on the table for the shot. This was a very short photo session."
Mrs. Philippe Halsman

John Bryson
Ketcham, Idaho
1958
"Hemingway was sitting at the kitchen counter, drinking wine, and his cat just wandered in and jumped up into the picture."

Eva Rudling
Françoise Sagan
Normandie, France
1978

Photographer Unknown
Paris
1930's

"Our perfect companions never have fewer than four feet," wrote Colette, one of a select group of writers of her time, who cherished, as connoisseur and companion, the secret friendship of cats. Never was her love for her feline friends more apparent than in her writings: the "Pegots" cats of the Mont-Boucons, the cats of Claudine, and the cats of the Rue de Courcelles. La Chatte Dernière, the last of Colette's many cats, died in February 1939, and her devotion to it was such that, in tribute to her friend, she eschewed all successors until her death, at the age of 81, in 1954.

Philippe Halsman
Dali Atomicus
1958
"Mr. Halsman had the idea of photographing Dali in the air, because of Dali's belief in the atom—in his paintings nothing touches the ground—so we rented three cats and worked with four assistants.
One assistant was throwing the water, and three were throwing the cats, and all of it had to be timed so that everything could move at the same time. Dali had to jump; the cats had to be in the air; the water had to splash. Mr. Halsman did this shot twenty-six times. After each time, he would go up in the darkroom and develop the four-by-five film. He'd return, saying, 'No, no. It isn't working out. Something is wrong. The water doesn't hit the cats, or the cats are not visible.'
After each shot we had to wipe up the studio and get hold of the cats. Dali and Mr. Halsman were exhausted. The cats were limp. After that, I fed them all some Portuguese sardines, and they were very happy."
Mrs. Philippe Halsman

Jean-Regis Roustan
Paris
1975
André Malraux—at the time he gave a famous interview on behalf of his cat to the magazine *L'Express*. Claudine Vernier-Palliez, the reporter, recalls, "He loved his cats, but he was afraid of them. When he died, they spent days howling."

Jill Krementz
Key West
1972
Tennessee Williams, with friend, by a swimming pool.

Fat Cats

Almost all of us know that you can't be too rich or too thin. All of us, that is, except the fat cats.

When photographer Bill Hayward went searching for the fattest cats, he discovered that they were easier to photograph than their thinner brothers and sisters. Reason: Fat cats just don't move around a lot. Put them in a comfortable place—a plush satin comforter, a nice cool sink on a hot summer's day, or a pile of cashmeres in a closet—and they'll just curl up and hold the pose for hours.

Hayward also unearthed the existence of a loosely connected grapevine of fat cat owners. One conversation with one owner invariably led to the name of another, and so on. And, remarkably, most of the conversations seemed to follow the same pattern: Bill's initial question would be answered with a short pause and then laughter.

Most owners of fat cats don't consider their pets to be fat—just big. Veterinarians feel, however, that like their human counterparts, some cats are simply genetically disposed to obesity, and others, alas, like their masters and mistresses, just LOVE food.

Bill Hayward
New York
1979
"This is Michael O'Donoghue's cat, Willis. He's very indolent and reads a lot of movie magazines to keep up with his favorite stars."

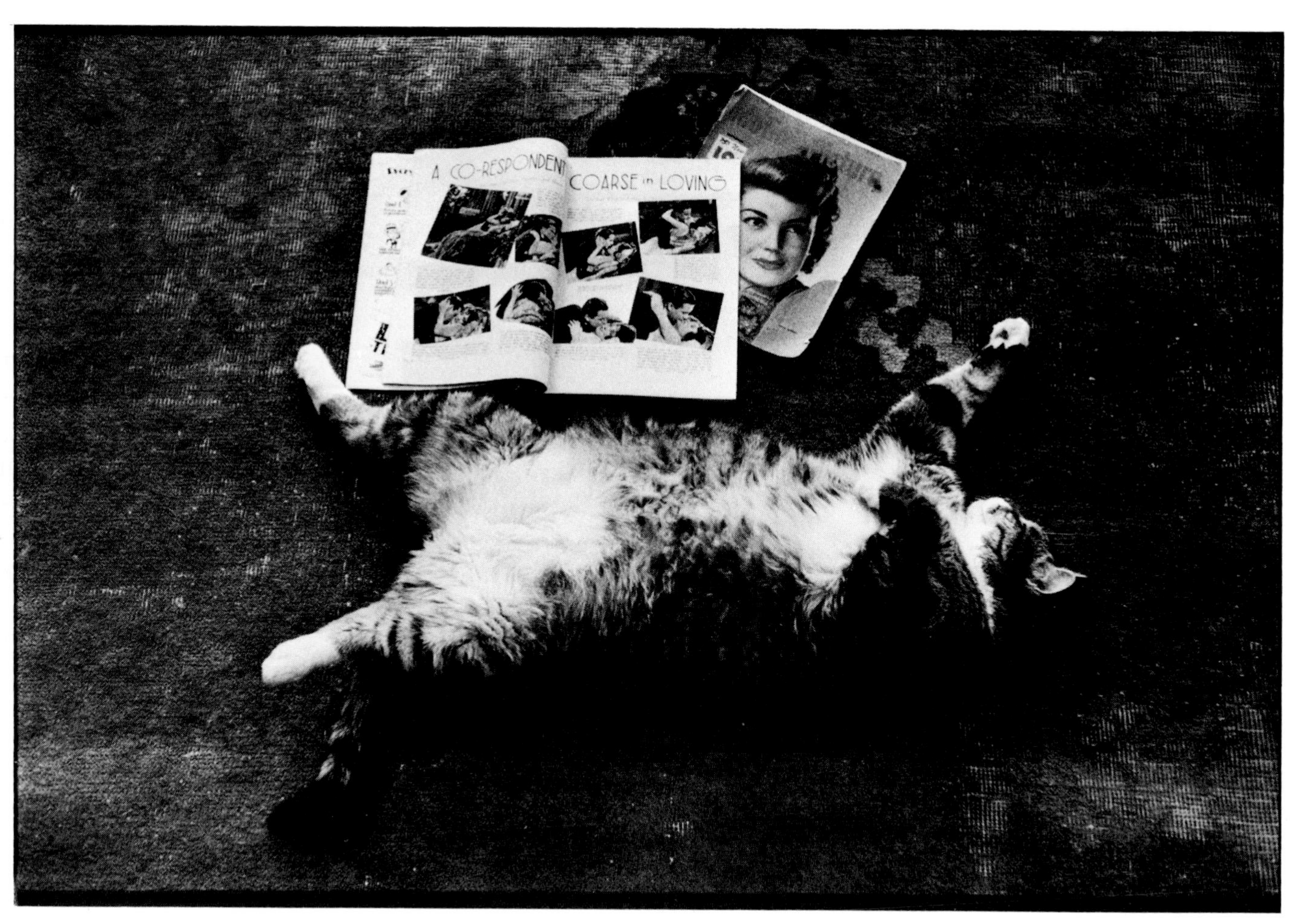
A CO-RESPONDENT
COARSE in LOVING

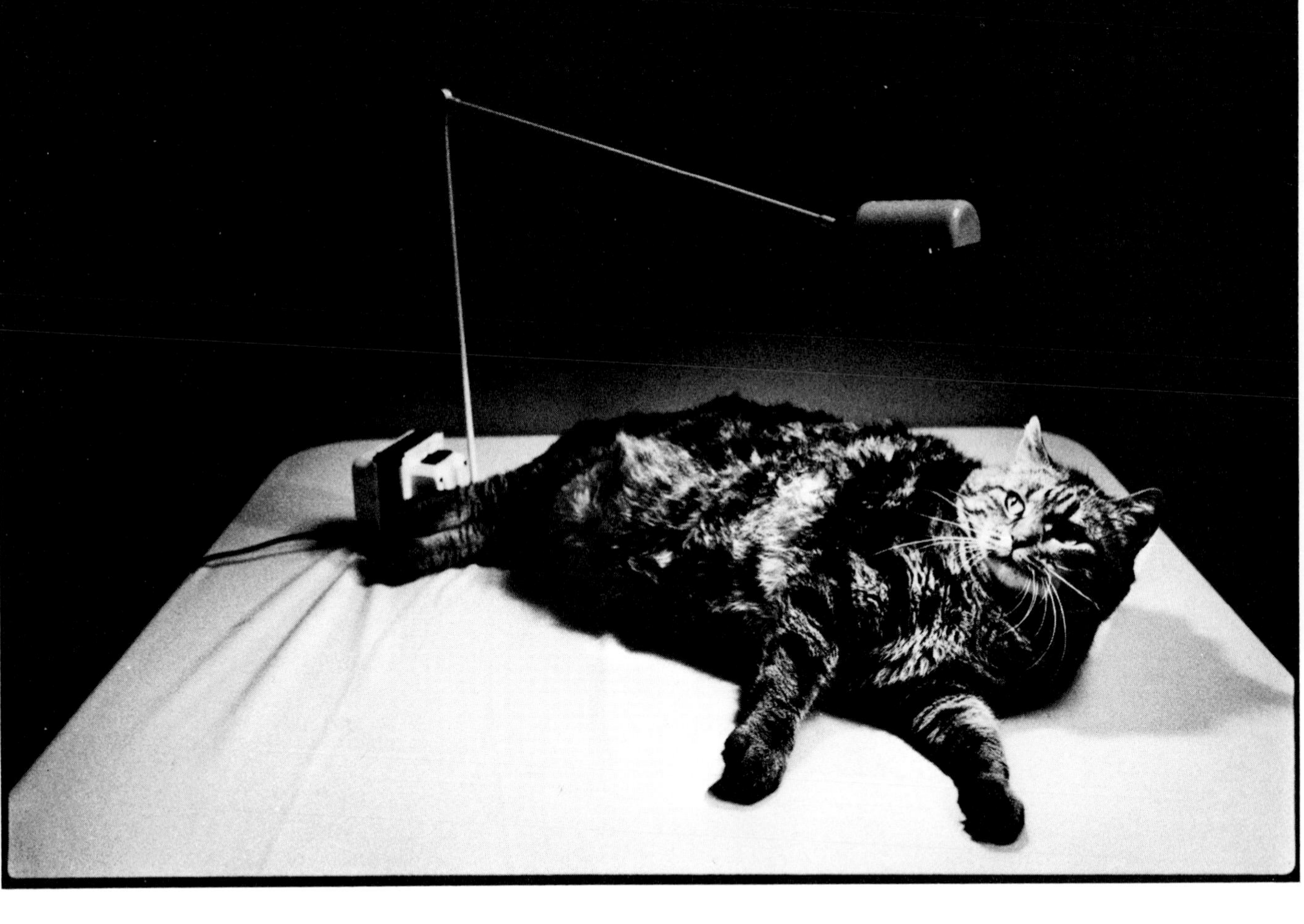

Bill Hayward
New York
1978
"Fats doesn't move real fast. This picture of him was taken at his owner's apartment. This is his own little spa area—his answer to the Golden Door—complete with his own little heat lamp and massage table."

Bill Hayward
New York
1979
"Cow is a television addict. His owner, Michael O'Donoghue, used to write for *Saturday Night Live*."

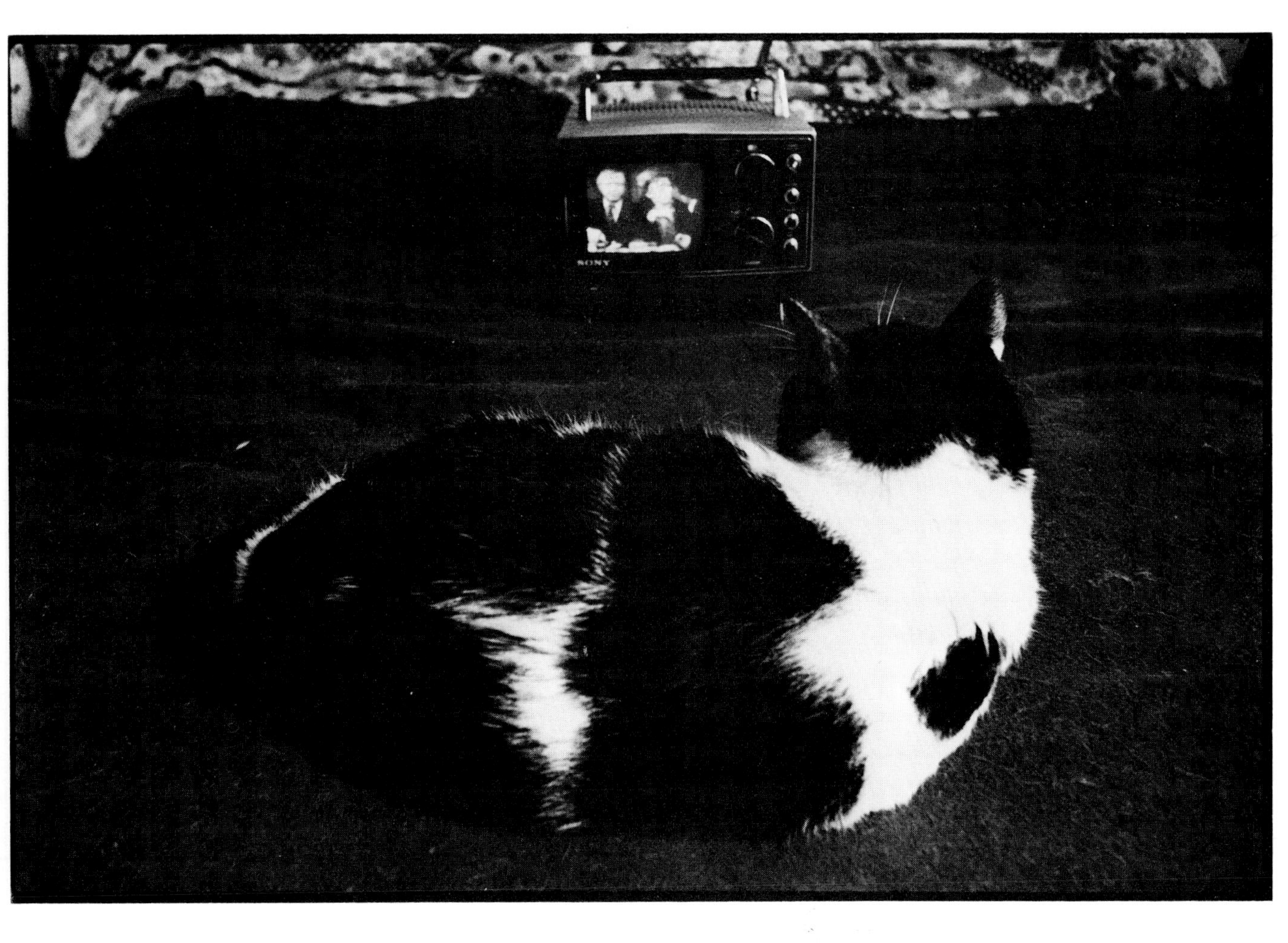

Following Pages:

Bill Hayward
New York
1979
"This is one of Cow's favorite places to be. It's always cool, and it's the one place big enough to contain him."

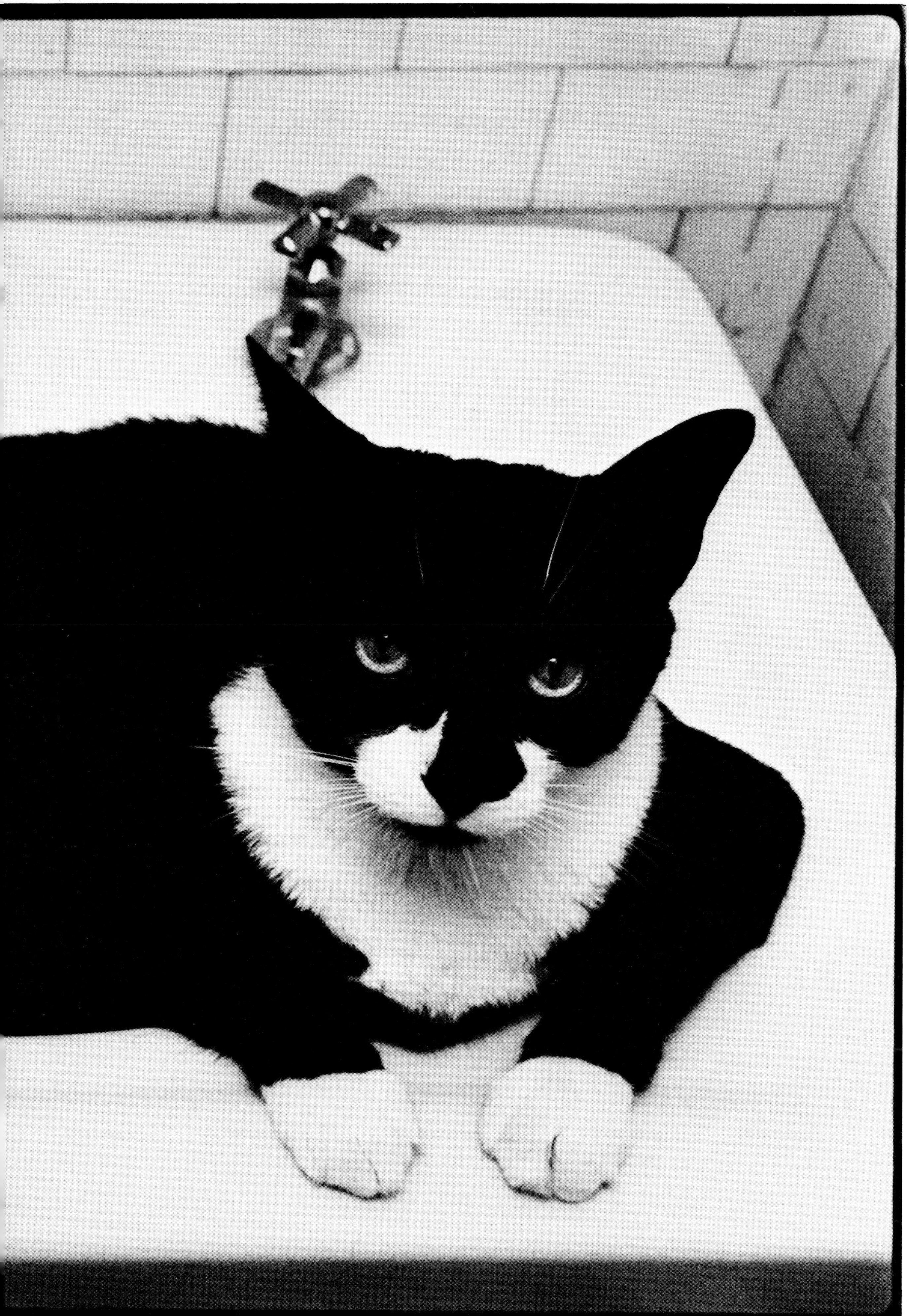

Acknowledgements

Front Cover: © Peter B. Kaplan
Back Cover: © Jere Cockrell
2-5: Ylla, Photoresearchers, Inc.
6: Thomas Eakins, The Metropolitan Museum of Art, David H. McAlpin Fund, 1943
9: The Bettmann Archive, Inc.
10-11: Harry Frees, The Rotograph Company, courtesy of Arthur Tress
12-13: Eadweard Muybridge, courtesy of the American Museum of Natural History
14: Ylla, Photoresearchers, Inc.
15: © 1979, Barbara Morgan
16: Associated Press
17: © Jill Freedman
18-19: N.Y. Daily News Photo
20: The Bettmann Archive, Inc.
21: United Press International
22: © Priscilla Rattazzi
23: © Roy Morsch
24: © Jill Krementz
25: © Courtesy of Daniel J. Edelman, Inc.
26: © Frank Spinelli (top) © Ed Centner (bottom)
27: © 1975, Ralston-Purina Company (top)
28: © Arthur Tress
29: © 1980, Sterling Publishing Co., Inc.
31: © Jill Freedman
32: © André Kertesz
33: © 1980, Ruth Orkin
34-35: © André Kertesz
36-37: © 1980, Ruth Orkin
38: © 1976, Philippe Salaün
39: © 1979, Harvey Stein
40-41: Henri Cartier-Bresson, © Magnum Photos, Inc.
42-43: © André Kertesz
44: © Eleni Mylonas
45: © Jill Freedman
46: © Jill Freedman
47: © Brian Lav
48: © Jim Bengston
49: © Rick Smolan
50-51: Elliott Erwitt © 1968, Magnum Photos, Inc.
52-53: © Jane Shreibman
55: © William Coupon
56: © Eleni Mylonas
57: © Diane Marino
58-59: © Jill Krementz
60-61: © Duane Michals
62: From the Collection of Allan H. Orenstein
63: David Seymour, © Magnum Photos, Inc.
64-65: Bruce Davidson © Magnum Photos, Inc.
66: © Susan Opton
67: © Jill Freedman
68: © Jill Freedman
69: © Terry Gruber
70: © Barbara Alper
71: © Antonio Mendoza
73: © Brian Lav
74: From the Collection of Allan H. Orenstein
75: Edward Steichen, courtesy of the Museum of Modern Art, Collection of Mr. and Mrs. Noel Levine, used by permission
76-77: © Susan Chang
78: © Liza Himmel
79: © Matthew Klein
80: © Arthur Tress
81: © George A. Tice
82: © Antonio Mendoza
83: © Jill Freedman
84-85: © Dan Wynn
86: © Armen Kachaturian
87: © Anthony Loew
88: © Carol Weinberg
89: © 1979, Lawrence Robins
90: © Antonio Mendoza
91: © Jean C. Pigozzi
92: © Carol Weinberg
93: © Jill Freedman
94-95: © André Kertesz
96: © Jane Shreibman
97: The Bettmann Archive, Inc.
98: © Peter B. Kaplan
99: © 1979, Barbara Morgan
100-101: © Carl Fisher
102-103: © Antonio Mendoza
104: Leonard Freed © Magnum Photos, Inc.
105: Guy Le Querrec © Magnum Photos, Inc.
106: © Rick Smolan
107: © Eleni Milonas
108: Réunion des Musées Nationaux, Paris
109: © Jill Krementz
110: © Arnold Newman
111: © Philippe Halsman
112-113: © John Bryson
114: © Eva Rudling, Sygma
115: © Roger-Viollet, Paris
116-117: © Philippe Halsman
118: Jean-Regis Roustan, L'Express, Paris
119: © Jill Krementz
121-125: © Bill Hayward
128: © Bill Hayward

Index to Photographers

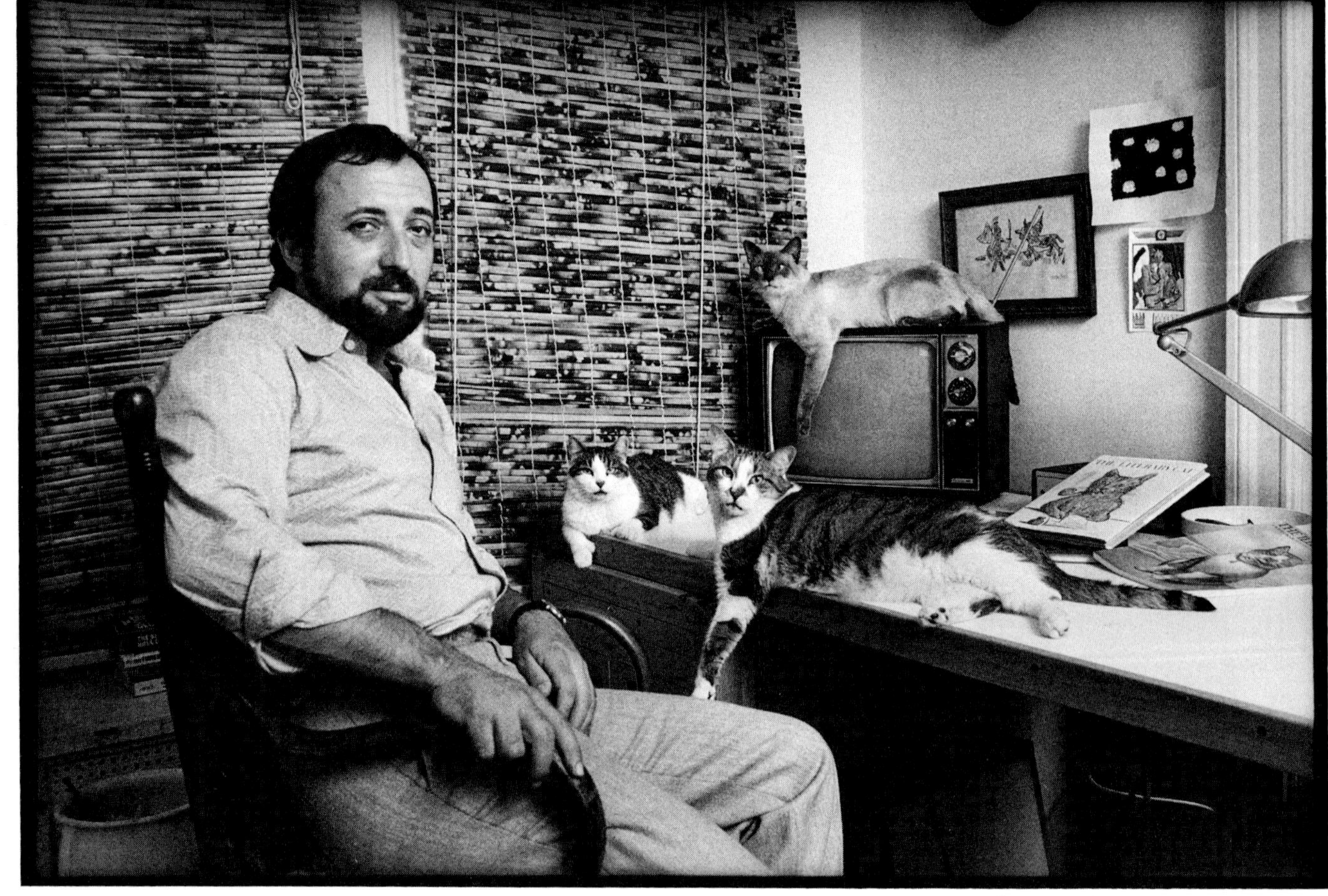

Bill Hayward
Portrait of the Author
New York
1978